Overcoming Common Problems

Depression:
Healing Emotional Distress

LINDA HURCOMBE

sheldon **PRESS**

First published in Great Britain in 2007

Sheldon Press
36 Causton Street
London SW1P 4ST

British Library Cataloguing-in-Publication Data
A catalogue record for this book is available from the British Library

ISBN 978-1-84709-014-0
1 3 5 7 9 10 8 6 4 2

Typeset by Fakenham Photosetting Ltd, Fakenham, Norfolk
Printed in Great Britain by Ashford Colour Press

Produced on paper from sustainable forests

For Trish Johnson, Susan Dowell and Dorothy Rowe
(Work is what we do, love is what we make)

Contents

Contents

Note to readers

This book contains the opinions and ideas of its author. It is intended to provide helpful and informative material on the subjects addressed in the publication. It is sold with the understanding that the author and publisher are not engaged in rendering medical, health, or any other kind of personal professional services in the book. The reader should consult his or her medical, health, or other competent professional before adopting any of the suggestions in this book or drawing inferences from it.

The author and publisher specifically disclaim all responsibility for any liability, loss, or risk, personal or otherwise, which is incurred as a consequence, directly or indirectly, of the use and application of any of the contents of this book.

The contacts and case histories described in this book are based on interviews and/or correspondence with real persons, and include people who have contacted the author for advice and correct information. The names, professions, and other details about the participants have been altered.

Note to readers

This book contains the opinions and ideas of its author. It is intended to provide helpful and informative material on the subjects addressed in the publication. It is sold with the understanding that the author and publisher are not engaged in rendering medical, health, or any other kind of personal professional services in the book. The reader should consult his or her medical, health, or other competent professional before adopting any of the suggestions in this book or drawing inferences from it.

The author and publisher specifically disclaim all responsibility for any liability, loss, or risk, personal or otherwise, which is incurred as a consequence, directly or indirectly, of the use and application of any of the contents of this book.

The contacts and case studies described in this book are based on interviews and/or correspondence with real persons, and include people who have contacted the author for advice and correct information. The names, professions and other details about the participants have been changed.

Acknowledgements

I want in this book to draft maps to explain, visualize and heal depression. I have discovered that there are many paths to recovery and that our journeys are of infinite variety. I am not a specialist in the field of depression; however, the circumstances of my life have required some serious attention to human suffering, and a passion to communicate what I have discovered. Most of us overcome depression without resort to mental health services; we do this by calling on inner resources, by reading and contemplation, friendship and love, work and play, religion, art, travel, animal companions, and the passage of time – just some of the infinite ways in which we refresh our spirits and learn to live with our losses.

Thank you to all the frankly magnificent people who gave permission to include your stories.

Thank you to my life partner, Trish Johnson. You stood by me through catastrophe and its aftermath. To the Johnson extended family, Pauline and Len, Kate and John Polson, Oliver and Paddy Polson, Louise and Randal Owles, Jack and Phillipa Owles – you all held me when I was broken. To my dear 'rellies' Auntie Ruth Mary, my brother Roy Gould and sister Nancy Roubanis, nephews Curt and Scott and spouses Anna and Trudi; you listened and offered wisdom.

Thank you to Susan Dowell, fearsome friend and co-author of the first book, to Josie Owen and Peter Thompson, Hillary and Lawrence Ratna, Mike and Linda McKeen, Ursula Freeman, Jill Gray, Ron Davies, Rhiannon, Catriona and Charles, Judy Harper, Angela Martin, Angela Clemson and Jo Withington, Val Bond and Betty Saunders, Caroline Price, Ron, Lynn, Amy and Luke Hester, Joyce Williams, Lisa Beznosiuk, Richard and Luba Mai Tunnicliffe, whose friendship and personal support are inestimable.

To David Healy, Charles Medawar, Dorothy Rowe, Andy Vickery, Paul Vincent. Vince Boehm, Freda Bonner, Yolande Clarke, Sarah Boseley, Cassandra Casey, Gill Goodwillie, Emma Holister, Catherine Jackson, Ramo Kabbani, Millie Kieve, Gordon Lamont, Pat Neil, Evelyn Pringle, Pete Postlethwaite, Vera Sharav, Shirley Trickett. To the bloggers, artists, psychiatrists, watchdogs, proofreaders, head-readers (as in 'I'm having my head read today') – your wisdom is the rocket fuel of this project.

Finally to Joanna Moriarty, editor and best critic, and to the editorial team, especially Louise Clairmonte and Kathryn Wolfendale. None of us will ever be rich, but you are the reason this book is out there. Thank you.

Foreword:
depression, wounding and healing

Depression today is often referred to as the common cold of psychiatry, but this is not how it used to be. Once depression was a much more serious illness, not readily confused with nerves or nervous breakdowns. But times were different then, and we must now face up to the current situation. People who are diagnosed with depression nowadays might be suffering from anything from old style 'nerves' or breakdowns to proper melancholia. Alternatively they may have problems stemming from their circumstances or be in the midst of a spiritual crisis. No one can readily tell. There are no blood tests to sort out these competing possibilities. Without the benefit of hindsight, not even an expert can tell you after the event whether it was reasonable to give you an antidepressant or not.

What you need if you go to your doctor, or even before you go, is a friend to pick things over with. And that is what Linda Hurcombe offers here. As will become clear to any reader, Linda has seen depression from pretty well all possible sides. Whatever depression is these days, it has assailed Linda herself and taken away those closest to her as she has looked on bewildered. The turmoil depression brought into her own life led her to turn her gaze on what was happening and set up a support line for others. These may be people caught up in the throes of a real illness, with the capacity to maim or kill, or perhaps those following a course of treatment for a condition 'created' by the medical profession, the end result of which could prove equally harmful. Her work supporting others led to many of the cases she describes in Chapter 5.

These case histories sit at the heart of this book. They hint at the many ways into and out of depression. They do not offer easy answers but they will leave most readers feeling that here is someone they could turn to if they needed support. Someone who would not only not force answers upon them, but who would also leave open spaces that are rarely left open by the doctors or psychologists to whom they might be referred these days.

We are passing through a difficult period. One in which 'myths' about what happens when people get depressed have taken hold, such as the idea that depression involves a lowering of serotonin. An era in which experts, who are supposed to protect us against such marketing myths put out by pharmaceutical companies, have instead been co-opted by these companies. An era in which these same companies have found it cheaper and more effective to use a professor of psychiatry to sell the product than to hire traditional drug reps. An era, therefore, in which conflicts of interest have become a serious issue in medicine.

These financial conflicts of interest unfortunately loom increasingly large for all of us. As a result, many patients are coming to realize that going to a doctor is much less safe than they once believed. There are, however, two more important conflicts than this. The first is to have suffered from an illness and to be committed to the mode of treatment that worked for you, and the second is to have had a family member injured by a treatment. How many of us would be able to recommend a treatment that had devastated our own lives? It is a rare person who can go through experiences like this and not emerge skewed or, even more significantly, who can use them to reach out to others. This is what Linda Hurcombe has done in this book.

This book is a wonderful resource and a voice of sanity for anyone facing depression, or for whom treatment seems not to be going to plan, or for anyone who is living with a depressed person.

Dr David Healy FRCPsych
Professor of Psychological Medicine
Cardiff University

Introduction

There is a third certainty in life in addition to death and taxes –
everyone gets depressed.

Depression is the most prevalent 'illness' in the Western world.
According to the World Health Organization depression will
become the world's second most pervasive debilitating condition
by the year 2020, second only to heart disease. Judging by statistics
you could be forgiven for thinking that we are a nation of depressives; indeed, according to a recent survey commissioned by the
British Association for Counselling and Psychotherapy, two-thirds
of British adults say they suffer from depression.

In 1993, 10.8 million courses of antidepressants were dispensed in the UK. Ten years later this number had almost trebled, with more than 27 million prescriptions for similar drugs being prescribed. People suffering from 'mild to moderate mental health problems' in the early years of the twenty-first century are prescribed drugs by overworked doctors as a quick-fix solution in response to patient demand and the pervasive lack of counselling services in the NHS, coupled with the stresses and isolations of contemporary life. In May 2006 health secretary Patricia Hewitt declared the end of the 'Prozac Nation', launching a programme to cut the numbers of patients on drugs such as Prozac and Seroxat and to extend counselling to the thousands of people with 'mild to moderate' depression and anxiety.

Like all ventures that matter, this book begins with love as its origin, journey and destination, in this case transcending personal tragedy. In 1998, the world crashed around family and friends when my healthy and undepressed 19-year-old daughter Caitlin hanged herself. She had been taking an antidepressant medication called Prozac for 63 days. In those days it was not known that this drug and its close relatives are clearly linked to suicide risk for a significant percentage of vulnerable people. She had heard from an uncle and from her own teen 'bush telegraph' that the drug was 'mega'. So she went to our local GP, said she was anxious about college, the boyfriend and arguing at home, and was prescribed the drug. Her behaviour changed immediately, and over subsequent weeks Caitlin descended into a chaotic world of self-harm and eventually violence, first towards others and then terminally, to herself.

Because Caitlin's behaviour changed so radically from the first day she was on the medication, I had suspicions early on, but with no evidence to back up my thoughts. Although we had experienced serious loss and suffering, depression was not a condition known in our family and I had little understanding about its nature. However, initially I thought Caitlin must have been suffering from an undiagnosed depressive state. Subsequent research over intervening years has revealed an unpalatable but irrefutable fact. One of a significant 'subpopulation', Caitlin had a toxic fatal reaction to one of the world's most popular drugs.

Advocates of the medical model of the condition claim that depression is a physical illness, like diabetes or bacterial infection, most likely deriving from a lack of the chemical serotonin. This position evolved in the second half of the twentieth century. Historically depression has been thought of as resulting from stress, or from a lack of wisdom in living and self-knowledge, or from intense unhappiness and sadness resulting often from the loss of a relationship, or the inability to sustain a loving relationship, and loss of purpose or meaning in life (Rowe, 2001). In past generations people tended to accept that they would spend a significant time being unhappy because life was very difficult. In its more extreme manifestations depression and mania, along with other socially unusual behaviours, have traditionally even been seen as a form of demon possession, or an 'infection' of the soul.

Modern life may be stressful, but infinitely better than in 'the old days', or so we are taught. We are also taught to expect more from life than our forebears might have done. We think we must have a great sex life and job and material things to be happy. It's not 'pukka' to admit we are unhappy, so instead we say we are depressed. If things get very rough we may consult our GP, wanting a name for our condition and a solution. The diagnosing of our 'condition' as depression, and prescribing antidepressant medication, fulfils both needs.

The medical model of depression is on many levels an attractive notion; it is, however, just one hypothesis of several, and some patients and medical experts are sceptical of the simplistic idea that depressed people have defective brains, or for that matter are genetically predestined to suffer the condition. One need only ask recipients of antidepressant medication what sort of test their doctor conducted on their behalf to conclude that they have a chemical deficiency. No such test exists, and the only point at which serotonin levels can be confirmed is at autopsy.

The longer holistic view contends that depression is a 'legitimate emotional response to life's difficulties and inseparable from individuality, race, colour, gender, creed, upbringing, belief systems, environments, relationships, socio-economic factors, life events and coping skills' (Corry and Tubridy, 2005). The nature of depression is to rob us of the very qualities (faith, inner strength, energy, desire) necessary for a recovery. On this level it is a very clever condition in its capacity for destructiveness. Adherents of the holistic model contend that isolating us from our thoughts and behaviours, and from the workings of our world, is a dangerous practice, that the sick-brain model of depression ... turns people into 'cogs in a machine where, if we find the going difficult and need to disengage, our distress is silenced by a [mind-altering drug] ... and we are encouraged to carry on regardless' (Corry and Tubridy, 2005). Thus do many of us unwittingly commit ourselves to becoming permanent patients.

This book explores the experience of depression and coping with it, and offers solid strategies for recovery and well-being. An important strength of this approach derives from standing alongside those suffering the pain of depression, in the positive, clear and supportive style characteristic of my book *Losing a Child: Explorations in Grief* (Sheldon Press, 2004), and in presenting material as a sympathetic personal dialogue between author and reader – 'we' and 'you', rather than 'they' and 'them'. This style does not preclude vigorous debate, and readers will readily see that some of the issues in this book represent impassioned arguments conducted both with myself and with informed colleagues, as a result of continuing peer counselling, research and personal experience. Any elements of campaigning for improvements in mental health services are intentional and vital.

The chapters include stories of depression and healing from people I have worked with or have invited to contribute. Balance is crucial, but it would be a mistake to avoid taking a stand based on the best available information, namely that the disease-medication model for treating depression is less helpful than one would hope. Reliable clinical trials continue to affirm that friendship, talking about feelings, counselling, community support, diet, exercise, breathing techniques and particularly placebos have been found to be as effective as medication for the treatment of depression (see Chapter 6). Importantly, because antidepressant medications have sometimes life-threatening side effects, they should be used only in extreme cases and with the greatest caution. My position would not recommend the abolition of these medications; rather, I commend a more straightforward and widely available body of information for medical practitioners and public alike, comprehensive safety testing, cautious prescribing, regular monitoring and, crucially, effective regulation of pharmaceutical companies' clinical trial reporting and marketing strategies.

The following pages provide the most reliable and up-to-date information available – with fresh perspectives, skills and resources with which to live through and manage depression, as well as equipping us to be a helpmate when friends or family members seek healing and recovery. I have included spiritual discussions which have proven helpful to people burdened and sometimes immobilized by depression.

I believe depression is caused by feelings of lovelessness, fear, abandonment, loneliness, powerlessness, anger, loss of hope and despair. No single 'cure' can be comprehensive. Virtually every case of depression has, as part of the complex web of causes, the loss of a relationship. Although every mood and bodily function is processed in the brain, these very human emotions cannot be explained away by chemical changes alone, or helped in any enduring way by swallowing drugs. Rather than being a mental disorder, depressive states are part of what we call 'the human condition'. Like the late M. Scott Peck, author of *The Road Less Travelled*, I am old-fashioned enough to hesitate to presume an airtight division between what we call 'mental' and what we call 'spiritual'.

The term 'psychiatry' traditionally means 'study of the soul', dealing with mental, emotional and behavioural disorders. Inserting God into any psychiatric equation is often considered unusual and even dangerous. I know of more than one psychiatrist who admits to loving magic, but avoids the subject of God like the plague. Readers interested in spirituality will be encouraged to consider the place of faith in the context of how faith can affect/affirm and heal a person who is depressed.

Just as we need vocational, recreational, social and artistic dimensions to our lives, we need a spiritual dimension to be whole. George Santayana once said the truly religious love what good life there is, making life worth living, and that our sense of what makes life worth living is very much derived from our religious traditions in their diversity, if and when we are lucky enough to have them.

Although I have had some medical and counselling training, I am an amateur in the field. By 'amateur' I mean 'lover'. I contacted psychiatrists and counsellors for advice when writing this book. I owe them a huge debt. I asked why as a peer advocate I was being treated with such respect. One reply sticks in my mind: 'You can get away with saying things that we can't. You can take the best from several differing specializations. You can mix science with ancient wisdom and even discuss the "f" word, i.e. faith. You aren't anti-doctor and you're not anti-homespun cures.'

In these pages are some stories and histories, tools for healing, covering the full range of concerns in a sound way and 'bite-size' format, for those of us who suffer depression, and for those of us who want to help the sufferer – family members, friends, physicians, counsellors.

1

How it feels to be depressed: the black dog

The beauty of love has not found me
Its hands have not gripped me so tight
For the darkness of hate is upon me
I see day, not as day, but as night.

I yearn for the dear love to find me
With my heart and my soul and my might
For darkness has closed in upon me
I see day, not as day, but as night.

The children are playing and laughing
But I cannot find love in delight
There is an iron fence all around me
I see day, not as day, but as night.

(Anonymous)

As a dog lover I am not alone in being intrigued by Winston Churchill's metaphorical naming of his own deep depression as his 'black dog'. Dogs inhabit extreme realms of the imagination – hounds of heaven, hounds of hell. Historically they have been sacred to many societies, representing both natural instinct and a bridge to life after death. They are also purported to be our courageous, unconditional best friend. Yet like all best friends they can turn on us and hurt us. But if we have trained and nurtured them, we know how to bring them back in line, tame them, even lock them up for a time if necessary, reminding them who is 'Alpha' dog.

The hallmarks of depression

Is depression a self-constructed prison? Are we the architects of an 'iron fence' around ourselves and within our own thoughts, no matter how 'dysfunctional' or 'weird'? Is it enough to find alternative ways of thinking in order to free us, or if not free, to give us scope for a fuller and more positive life? Will we need to seek professional help to feel whole again?

I dislike dithering, but the most accurate answer appears to be yes. And no. Depression is a state of being which can paralyse, debilitate and destroy relationships. Although more marked in developed countries, the hallmarks of such emotional despair appear to be universal, timeless and consistent. These hallmarks are many and varied:

- exhaustion
- loss of self-esteem
- a sense of being in a fog
- insomnia or its opposite
- eating too little or too much
- loss of motivation and energy
- times of restless uncomfortable activity
- despair
- selfishness and inability to support friends
- introversion and compulsive self-analysis
- too much alcohol

Let's discuss our feelings, shall we?

- recklessness, e.g. gambling
- inability to socialize
- inability to feel pleasure
- reckless spending
- lack of concentration
- suicidal feelings
- paranoia.

More direct physical symptoms can accompany depression and its flip-side, anxiety:

- loss of interest in sex
- tight chest or throat
- shaking
- dizziness
- wind
- breathing difficulties
- pumping heart
- excessive sweating
- swallowing problems
- weight loss/gain
- headaches
- tinnitus (ringing in the ears)
- aching all over.

Depression deemed to require professional intervention is called 'clinical depression'. The symptoms that help a doctor identify our distress as needing treatment include:

- constant feelings of sadness, irritability or tension;
- decreased interest or pleasure in usual activities or hobbies;
- loss of energy, feeling tired despite lack of activity;
- change in appetite, with significant weight loss or weight gain;
- change in sleeping patterns, such as difficulty sleeping, early morning awakening, or sleeping too much;
- restlessness or feeling slowed down;
- decreased ability to make decisions or concentrate;
- feelings of worthlessness, hopelessness or guilt;
- thoughts of suicide or death.

Toleration of our depressive states often provokes witty responses. I quote an example from an audio-email forwarded to me by a 'blog friend':

> Hello and welcome to the Mental Health hotline.
> If you're obsessive-compulsive, press 1 repeatedly.
> If you are co-dependent, ask someone to press 2 for you.
> If you have multiple personalities, press 3, 4, 5 and 6.
> If you are paranoid, we know what you are, and what you want
> – stay on the line and we'll trace your call.
> If you're delusional, press 7 and your call will be transferred to
> the mother ship.
> If you're schizophrenic, listen carefully and a small voice will
> tell you which number to press.
> If you're dyslexic, press 6 9 6 9 6 9 6 9 …
> If you have a nervous disorder please fidget with the hash key
> until the beep – after the beep, please wait for the beep.
> If you have short-term memory loss please try your call again
> later, and if you have low self-esteem hang up. All our
> operators are too busy to talk to you.
> And finally, if you're depressive it doesn't matter which number
> you press, no one will answer you.

I found this hilarious, but more than one friend to whom I forwarded the message chided me, saying that it represents the very intolerance and scornfulness regarding emotional distress that we should be trying both to address and to change.

Do I need medication?

Humour or the lack thereof aside, when depression hits our busy, stressed culture, we have perhaps tended to hit the bottle, either one containing alcohol, or one containing tablets. The introduction in the late 1980s of the new generation of 'magic bullet' antidepressants led to a euphoria about the efficacy of medication and a concomitant decline in the availability of counselling services within the NHS. Happily this situation is now altering. After all, pills can be quick and can seem to fit in with our fast-paced stressful lives. But does any quick fix work?

Apparently not. In May 2006, UK health secretary Patricia Hewitt formally announced a monumental shift of public policy for Britain, and the end of what she termed our 'Prozac Nation'. Noting that the prescription of 'happy pills' had risen by more than 12 per cent over the preceding decade, she declared public support for access to counselling and talk therapy (targeting CBT, or cognitive behavioural therapy, as particularly useful – see Chapter 6) for depressed people.

> Millions of people suffer from mild to moderate [*sic*] mental health problems, and treating them takes up about a third of a GP's time. Too many people are prescribed medication as a quick fix solution, but talking therapies work equally well and patients prefer to receive them. We know that people in work have better health than those out of work and the *Choosing Health* White Paper made clear that work matters – it can improve your mental and physical health, reduce health inequalities and improve life chances for people and their families.
>
> (<www.medicalnewstoday.com>, 16 May 2006)

Ms Hewitt went on to extol the economic wisdom of improving access to talking therapies ('saving millions of pounds') by helping people back to employment and off incapacity benefit, observing that a third of people on incapacity benefit in the UK suffer from 'mild to moderate' depression.

It is true that those of us experiencing depression and anxiety have for many years been offered little more than medication. In the United States it is now virtually impossible to obtain health insurance funding for counselling therapy. The trouble is that medication does not always help, and can indeed create unforeseen and harmful problems of dependency attended by addictive and debilitating side effects.

But am I sick if I am depressed? Psychologist Dorothy Rowe observes:

> This is the curious thing about depression. People call it an illness, but if you live with it you know it is not like any other illness. If someone you care about has a physical illness or an injury – bronchitis or cancer or a broken leg – you feel simple concern and sympathy for that person. You might feel anger at the injustices of life or at the carelessness of other people ... but you do

not find yourself possessed by a terrible rage with your loved one. Sick people can be querulous and difficult, but they do not turn on you and say hurtful, cruel things just as you are giving them extra love and comfort ... Having someone sick in the house can disrupt family routine, but sickness does not usually create a continual atmosphere of anger, mistrust and uncertainty. No matter how serious an illness is, you can come to understand it, and even if you do nothing but let the illness run its course, you can see the pattern and not feel as if you are the helpless victim of uncontrollable and dangerous forces ... but how can you be protected from the danger you feel of having a great well of despair open up in you? Being *with* a depressed person can be a very difficult and dangerous business.

(Rowe, 2001, my emphasis)

If depression is a disease, it is one which most if not all of us will be affected by during our lives, to varying degrees. One of the major problems with sufferers of 'malignant' or 'morbid' depression is that the very condition robs us of the belief that we can get better or that anyone else can possibly imagine the depths of our despair. The main energies of this book, however, point towards treating depression not as a disease but as widely experienced suffering and part of our human condition. It can be treated, and we can recover. As we shall see from the case studies in Chapter 5, some depressed people maintain that drug therapy helped. Others maintain that drug therapy was harmful, leading in some cases to serious problems of damage/dependency.

What we do know about talking, and other therapies, as alternatives to medication is that with a *competent* therapist, and/or a good friend, one can be helped and certainly no biological harm is done. For those of us without ready access to professional counselling, self-healing is possible, with some courage and imagination. Thus, my considered stance is that only in the most extreme forms of depression is medication advisable, alongside counselling and monitored with the utmost caution.

One extreme form of depression is bipolar disorder – in the past termed manic depression. Bipolar disorder falls into the serious and even 'morbid' end of the spectrum of depression. Kay Redfield Jamison is a professor of psychiatry in the United States who has suffered bipolar depression and specializes in this area of human distress – 'this quicksilver illness that can both kill and create'. Her popular memoir, *An Unquiet Mind: A Memoir of Moods and Madness*, tells us what it is like to be inside the head of a bipolar or manic-depressive person. She describes her own manias in their mild forms as 'absolutely intoxicating states that gave rise to great personal pleasure, and an incomparable flow of thoughts and a ceaseless energy'. Ideas and 'feelings are fast and frequent like shooting stars and you follow them till you find better, brighter ones. Shyness goes ... sensuality is pervasive and the desire to seduce and be seduced is irresistible.' But then comes the full-blown high when you are psychotic. You become 'irritable, frightened, angry, uncontrollable and enmeshed totally in the blackest caves of the mind. You never knew those caves were there. It will never end, for madness carves its own reality.' Then follows deep depression, the overdose, and the horrifying reminders of the extraordinary things you did when you were manic. Some people theorize that this distressing condition is genetic. The genetic component is a matter of intense and unresolved debate (see Chapter 4).

Am I really depressed?

How do we know when we are depressed rather than healthily sad? When someone I love dies or I fail to reach a much cherished goal, it is normal to feel sad. These feelings are quite profoundly a part of life, and my grief and sadness are complex, human and intricate. Depression is more complicated, and although just as human, almost always involves the following:

● a loss of belief in ourselves;
● a feeling that the depression will never ever go away;
● an inability to function productively;
● an inability to 'think straight' and a tendency to distorted thoughts.

I confess a wariness towards multiple-choice questionnaires as a tool of diagnosis, but discovered the following very useful checklist in a self-help book (Burns, 1990). Each question below is followed by four choices, that is: 0 = not at all; 1 = somewhat; 2 = moderately; 3 = a lot.

1 Sadness: have you been feeling sad or down in the dumps?
2 Discouragement: does the future look hopeless?
3 Low self-esteem: do you feel worthless or think of yourself as a failure?
4 Inferiority: do you feel inadequate or inferior to others?
5 Guilt: do you get self-critical and blame yourself for everything?
6 Indecisiveness: do you have trouble making up your mind about things?
7 Irritability and frustration: have you been feeling resentful and angry a good deal of the time?
8 Loss of interest in life: have you lost interest in your career, your hobbies, your family or your friends?
9 Loss of motivation: do you feel overwhelmed and have to push yourself hard to do things?
10 Poor self-image: do you think you're looking old or unattractive?
11 Appetite changes: have you lost your appetite? Or do you overeat or binge compulsively?
12 Sleep changes: do you suffer from insomnia and find it hard to get a good night's sleep? Or are you excessively tired and sleeping too much?
13 Loss of libido: have you lost your interest in sex?
14 Hypochondriasis: do you worry a great deal about your health?
15 Suicidal impulses: do you have thoughts that life is not worth living or think you (or others) would be better off – if you were dead? (Anyone with suicidal urges should seek immediate consultation with a qualified psychologist.)

Dr Burns shows readers how to diagnose moods using this checklist; there is also a similar checklist for people suffering from anxiety.

If you share my cynicism about multiple-choice questionnaires as a way of understanding complex human conditions, you may well be in good company. A number of people in my self-help group who completed multiple-choice questionnaires to diagnose their depressive state as a result spent months and in one case years being treated with a combination of antidepressant and other medications, only to discover that all along they were suffering from Lyme disease (a non-fatal bacterial infection transmitted by ticks, sometimes also misdiagnosed as myalgic encephalomyelitis or ME), which is treatable with antibiotics.

Thanks to public watchdogs and finally government intervention, the limitations and risks of antidepressant medications are now in the public domain, but this is a relatively recent state of affairs. In November 2001, with the help of an expert in dealing with problems arising from adverse effects of treatment of depression by medication, I set up a telephone/email self-help support group for people needing informed advice about side-effect problems ranging from tremors to akathisia (a highly unpleasant form of extreme restlessness, solely related to drug use). There is no website, and the address is passed on by personal recommendation and through reliable media helplines like the BBC. I named it 'Prozac and antidepressants alert networks'. The objectives were simple: to create a network of concerned people; to provide solidarity for the growing number of people affected by adverse reactions to the drugs, including the unexpected problems emerging when people tried to stop taking them; and to pool and disseminate information as it evolved on negotiating oneself through withdrawal (euphemistically referred to as 'discontinuation syndrome'). PANTS.UK (pants.uk@virgin.net) continues to provide reliable email and telephone support to all who make contact. (I am now convinced that another acronym would have been preferable; the one I chose derives from a contemporary joke which calls anything useless or harmful 'pants' – as in 'You may like that song but as far as I'm concerned it's a load of old pants.' In addition, a good acronym should relate to the subject matter. Never mind.)

Sadness and depression

Sadness and depression are different. When we are depressed, both joy and sadness elude us. Sadness, though, is a healthy emotion. It helps us adjust to significant loss. As our energy and enthusiasm for life's activities drop, sadness gives us the opportunity to mourn a loss or frustrated hope, and to understand its consequences in our life. The stronger the longing for what or who was lost, the more intense and uninhibited will be our weeping. It is in this release that our sadness can be transformed into a relieving and healing experience. Sadness is not the opposite of happiness. It is one of the myriad ways in which we respond from our whole self to what life brings. It is a path towards healing life's hurts.

2

A walk with the black dog through Western history

And yet in certain of these cases there is mere anger and grief and sad dejection of mind ... those affected with melancholy are not every one of them affected according to one particular form but they are suspicious of poisoning or flee to the desert from misanthropy or turn superstitious or contract a hatred of life. Or if at any time a relaxation takes place, in most cases hilarity supervenes. The patients are dull or stern, dejected or unreasonably torpid ... they also become peevish, dispirited and start up from a disturbed sleep.

(Arateus, 150 CE)

Neither neuroscientists nor psychiatrists can say exactly what depression is. Neurologically, psychologically, and historically, what Hippocrates called the 'black bile' and Susan Sonntag 'melancholy minus its charms' presents a truly complicated puzzle.

(David Dobbs, 'A Depression Switch?',
New York Times, 2 April 2006)

Evidence of depression from ancient times

The Egyptian Ebers Papyrus (*c.* 1550 BCE) is one of the oldest medical documents in the world, and contains a short description of depression. It is full of incantations and foul applications to turn away demons.

The terms *mania* and *melancholia* date from the Greeks, and numerous pictures of the condition appear in the classics as well as in the Bible. To the Greeks, mania referred to any overactive mental malady, and melancholia to any underactive state. It is possible that the manias were delirium, and the melancholias variants of Parkinson's disease or hypothyroidism.

My own culture and background draws me to the Bible, with the eloquence of its noble and suffering depressives. King Saul took his

11

life when depressed; and the blinded, enslaved and shackled Samson died by suicide with thousands of Philistines as he dislodged the pillars of their temple: 'Lord Yahweh, I beg you, remember me ... let me be revenged on the Philistines' (Judges 16.28, Jerusalem Bible (JB)).

Perhaps the most powerful evocation of biblical depression and grief appears in the book of Job. Job is a righteous and prosperous man. Satan requests of God that Job has all his good fortune swept away: wealth, children, house, even his physical health – everything precious to him. Even his wife chides, 'Curse God and die', and he is plagued by fair-weather 'comforters' whose observations are largely a form of spiritual torture for Job:

> I have been allotted months of futility, and nights of misery have been assigned to me. When I lie down I think, 'How long before I get up?' The night drags on, and I toss until dawn ... My days are swifter than a weaver's shuttle, and they come to an end without hope. Remember, O God, that my life is but a breath; my eyes will never see happiness again. The eye that now sees me will see me no longer ... I despise my life; I would not live for ever. Let me alone; my days have no meaning.
>
> (Job 7.3–4, 6–8, 16, New International Version (NIV))

Faced with the destruction of everything and nearly everyone he loved, this righteous man ponders the perennial problem of human suffering. The only 'answer' which arrives at the end is the entirely mysterious majesty of God and the enduring power of human love. The book of Job concludes with the restoration of his good fortune and family.

Job's depressed state arose from a clear cause, and his biblical companions, spanning the centuries, form an illustrious list. The psalmist, ascribed by tradition to King David, was eloquent in describing depression:

> My life is worn out with sorrow, my years with sighs; my strength yields under misery, my bones are wasting away. To every one of my oppressors I am contemptible, loathsome to my neighbours, to my friends a thing of fear. Those who see me in the street hurry past me; I am forgotten, as good as dead in their hearts, something discarded.
>
> (Psalm 31.10–12, JB)

Further, the psalmist bewails God's abandonment: 'It is you, God, who are my shelter: why do you abandon me? Why must I walk so mournfully, oppressed by the enemy? ... Why so downcast, my soul, why do you sigh within me?' (Psalm 43.2, 5a, JB).

Later the psalmist cries out that he is in deep water:

> Save me, God! The water is already up to my neck! I am sinking in the deepest swamp, there is no foothold; I have stepped into deep water and the waves are washing over me ... Do not let the waves wash over me, do not let the deep swallow me or the Pit close its mouth on me ... every one of my oppressors is known to you; the insults have broken my heart, my shame and disgrace are past cure; I had hoped for sympathy, but in vain, I found no one to console me.
>
> (Psalm 69.1–2, 15, 19–20, JB)

The book of Ecclesiastes is ascribed, probably as a literary device, to David's son Solomon (who was proverbially gifted with great wisdom) and opens with these plaintive words:

> Vanity of vanities, Qoheleth says. All is vanity! For all his toil, his toil under the sun, what does man gain by it? ... I thought to myself, 'Very well, I will try pleasure and see what enjoyment has to offer'. And there it was: vanity again! ... I resolved to have my body cheered with wine, my heart still devoted to wisdom; I resolved to embrace folly to see what made mankind happy, and what men do under heaven in the few days they have to live ... I then reflected on all that my hands had achieved and on all the effort I had put into its achieving. What vanity it all is, and chasing of the wind! There is nothing to be gained under the sun.
>
> (Ecclesiastes 1.2, 3, 2.1–3, 11, JB)

Isaiah addresses the tribe of Judah, a society beleaguered with what appears to be pervasive societal ill-doing and depression on an epic scale: 'The whole head is sick, the whole heart grown faint; from the sole of the foot to the head there is not a sound spot: wounds, bruises, open sores not dressed, not bandaged, not soothed with oil' (Isaiah 1.5b–6, JB).

Narratives in the four Gospels of the Christian testament tended to the view of demon possession curable by Jesus, and with miracles. I have heard it said that Jesus clearly suffered from depression when he spent 40 days fasting in the wilderness, as well as curing sufferers in his wider ministry.

The Greeks searched for explanations of both physical and psychological states. Empedocles (490–430 BCE) developed a theory of the humours: he taught that everything in existence is composed of four underived and indestructible roots, particles he identified as earth, air, fire and water. He believed that all illnesses were prompted by an imbalance among these humours. Hippocrates (460–377 BCE), considered with Galen the father of modern Western medicine, applied Empedocles' theory to mental disorders, insisting on natural causes for all illness and aberration. It was Hippocrates who importantly observed that 'Life is short; the Art is long'.

Plato (427–347 BCE) theorized two types of madness based on mysticism. The first sort of madness came from gods and conferred prophetic powers; the second sort was diseased. This second type happened when the irrational part of the human soul separated from the rational. This gulf caused an excess of happiness, sadness or pleasure-seeking. Plato saw these abandonments coming from an imbalance of the 'humours'. His pupil Aristotle (384–322 BCE) extended Plato's bipartite soul, musing that reason was immortal and therefore immune to illness. Therefore all illness, mental or not, was rooted in human physical structure.

The Romans came to dominate much of the 'civilized' world, but produced relatively few notable theorists. As in their architecture they apparently imported Greeks for necessary medical treatments. Many of these physicians settled in Rome, and Roman thinking about mental disorders tended to be an extension of Greek tradition. Galen (30–90 CE) was perhaps the most notable of these. Physician to Marcus Aurelius, he pioneered hugely important discoveries about the human body, and believed that mental disorders arose from an affliction of the brain, either directly or because it was affected by a problem in another bodily organ.

By the fourth century Christianity had moved, thanks to Constantine, from a persecuted minority to become the official religion of the by then ailing Roman empire. It is fair to say in a summary like this that the Church came to play a crucial role in bringing consolation to the masses. Supernatural explanations of mysterious phenomena were the norm. For a long time the scientific thinking of the Graeco-Roman era was lost, although earlier learning was accessible primarily in monasteries. Nunneries too were creative places of learning, healing and the arts. Records exist of herb and plant remedies to heal the sick. Sadly, unlike their pre-Christian pagan predecessors, women came to be seen as inferior and unclean. Despite this cost, abbesses sometimes held positions of great power.

In the sixth century the prophet Muhammad effected a religious transformation among the Bedouins. Within a century, the Arabs had conquered Babylonia, Persia, Syria and Egypt, and moved as far into Europe as Spain. This highly civilized culture brought back the medical practices of the Greeks, and during this time those who governed built hospitals for the insane. The Qur'an came to be seen as the authority for all knowledge. In Western Europe the mentally ill received treatment mainly from clerics. The harsh treatment, torture and executions of witches and sorcerers followed on, sparked off by the attitudes and times that spawned the Crusades and later the Inquisition.

Some argue that a form of demonology became the 'psychiatry' of the day. It is fair to presume that, through the centuries of phlegms and witch-hunts and wars – normal nasty mammal behaviour – we still struggled to understand how to treat depression. It is also not unreasonable to believe that sufferers of depression often escaped public opprobrium and the awfulness of being locked away because of the private nature of many manifestations of depression. In addition, the main purpose of early treatments would be the restraint (rather than rehabilitation) of behaviours considered a threat to society. Having written the previous sentences I realize that countless people today labelled with mental health conditions continue to be treated similarly, with the parameters of what constitutes normality being culturally and socially contingent.

People suffering from hearing voices, delusions, hallucinations, or periods of mania were more likely to be noticed in the overcrowded and cramped conditions of large cities, and there most often those with depression were locked away. Others in rural areas might remain unseen. But depression was, and is, more often than not a hidden state – those affected become self-involved, solitary, uncommunicative, spending much of the day asleep or solitary in a room.

Thus, if spared the horrors of being locked up as a 'lunatic' (a word deriving from the belief that mental disturbance was connected to the phases of the moon), the sufferer might have been left to dwell in relative silence and despairing of the possibility of a cure.

Towards the close of the fifteenth century psychological, legal and religious phenomena tended to be viewed as connected, and the devil was the repository of all ills. Mental aberration was equated with sin, and the devil's central obsession was sex. For sex, read female sex. The peerlessly infamous *Malleus Maleficarum*, or *Witch Hammer*, written by two Dominican priests and published in 1487, stated baldly that 'all witchcraft comes from carnal lust which is in women insatiable'. Some scholars maintain that as many as nine million people, almost all of them female, were exterminated during these terrible times. The term 'faggot' derives from the practice of binding male homosexuals with bundles, or faggots of wood, setting them alight and then using them as torches with which to burn female witches.

The beginnings of modern psychology and early treatments

The tide which began to turn away from such infamy is personified in the life of the Spanish humanist philosopher Juan Luis Vives (1492–1540), whose advanced thinking produced one of the first works of modern psychology. Vives helped establish hospitals for the treatment of mental patients and believed that people with mental health problems should be treated with the utmost humaneness.

The seventeenth century produced a great expansion of horizons both geographical and internal. Great explorers discovered new lands. Burton's *Anatomy of Melancholy* appeared in 1621. Spinoza (1632–77) theorized of the indivisibility of mind and body. He saw them as identical. He rejected the doctrine of absolute free will. Some historians see Spinoza's ideas as precursors to psychodynamics as well as Freud and Bleuler's formulation of ambivalence and Freud's view of repression.

One quickly discovers that, aside from the sort of 'case study' narratives we read in the Bible, the history of depression reveals little about what it is like to be depressed. Where depression was recognized, it tended to be thought of as a lesser concern, a lack of wisdom, lumped along with hypochondria and hysteria as 'the vapours', a 'nervous' or 'neurotic' complaint.

By the end of the eighteenth century, 'nerve doctors' proliferated into a thriving industry across Europe. In 1763 Pierre Pomme, who had been physician to the French king, claimed to have discovered the condition of 'vapours' among his wealthy clientele. Its symptoms? 'Fatigue, pain and a sense of dullness. Sadness, melancholy and discouragement poison all of their amusements.' Pomme's cure, for a condition that sounds suspiciously like the malaise of depression, was chicken soup and cold baths.

The opinion of doctors at this time appears to be that most forms of mental illness were due to disorders within the brain itself, although it was thought that the 'nervous' disorders, such as depression, anxiety and hypochondria, were not hereditary. 'The cause of madness is seated primarily in the blood vessels of the brain,' wrote the 'father' of American psychiatry Benjamin Rush in 1812, who saw all disease as springing from an excess of vascular activity (Healy, 1997). At one point and during an epidemic, Rush bled his entire family of twelve children twice a week, even his six-week-old baby. Other contemporaries developed complicated – and untested – theories around the notion that muscular spasms caused weakness in the blood vessels, and this in turn gave rise to various mental problems, including anxiety.

Social and cultural matters became important to those who took the view that mental illness was more a matter of nurture than nature. Factors such as one's family, upbringing, living conditions and employment were taken into account. In 1823 the German professor Johann Christian Heinroth gave a list of factors that could affect mental well-being: food, drink, sleep, exercise, air pollution. Few doctors working nowadays would deny that a poor diet, overindulgence in alcohol, lack of sleep and exercise, and an unhealthy environment can contribute to depression.

There was a strong sense that, whatever the causes, 'nervous' complaints like depression, phobias and chronic fatigue were not serious or life-threatening, and great effort was made to distinguish them from the sort of conditions that might lead to a person being confined to an asylum. Largely due to the justified public horror of these places, and their manifest inability to effect any sort of cure on the people locked up in them, mental illness was viewed with fear and loathing. However, 'nervous' complaints carried none of these negative associations – the upper and middle classes were quite happy to admit to suffering from them.

One solution for the wealthy would be a retreat to a spa town. In Britain, in spas like Bath or Cheltenham or Bognor Regis, melancholy and mania would be treated with a view to a cure.

In Europe during the nineteenth century, many sought the water cure, or hydrotherapy, and the spa towns there grew in popularity. Visitors firmly believed that drinking and bathing in waters rich in mineral deposits would bring relief. This turns out to be a sound practice – spa water is often rich in crucial trace elements needed for healthy living, such as iodine, potassium and iron. In addition the positive healing placebo effect, i.e. wanting a particular treatment to work and believing that it might help, would often be an important factor.

A disease vaguely resembling what we now call bipolar disorder was described as *folie circulaire* in 1850 by Falret and Baillarger in Paris (Healy, 2002), but American physicians rarely made the diagnosis before 1970.

Towards the end of the nineteenth century the first psychoactive drugs became available. The work of Emil Kraepelin (1855–1926) divided the major psychiatric disorders into manic-depressive illness and schizophrenia. Kraepelin also coined a term for the study of the effects of psychotropic drugs on psychological functioning: pharmacopsychology. The term used today is psychopharmacology, 'the science concerned with discovering the receptors that psychoactive drugs bind to, the levels they achieve in the brain and the benefits that these drugs offer to hospital services or general practitioners' (Healy, 2002).

The rise of psychoanalysis

Also towards the close of the nineteenth century, a number of practitioners began to experiment with hypnosis and the power of suggestion as a treatment for 'nervous' complaints, and this method influenced the work of Sigmund Freud, who believed that buried childhood memories were the cause of neuroses and depression in adult life. Freud worked without drugs, through a lengthy process of psychoanalysis. For 45 minutes a day, usually five times a week, the patient would lie on a couch, with the analyst positioned out of the patient's view. The patient would be encouraged to say whatever came into his or her mind, to use 'free association'. The idea was that, with the analyst's guidance, the unfulfilled desires and unresolved conflicts buried in the patient's subconscious mind would become conscious, and discussing these issues until the patient understood them would mean that they lost their power to cause deep distress and anxiety. Possibly the most lasting realization to come from Freud's technique was the idea that psychological and neurophysiological knowledge need not be contradictory. In other words, both biochemistry and psychology must be taken into account.

For some time, counselling and analysis proved more popular than 'biological' explanations looking for disturbances in the brain as a cause of the problems. Psychoanalysis gained favour as a treatment among the prosperous classes, first across Europe and then, as vast numbers of Europeans fled the Nazis during and after World War Two, in the USA. Along with other schools of psychotherapeutic thought, it proved so popular that many doctors believed manic depression and schizophrenia could be understood and treated with this method.

Early drug treatments for depression used at the beginning of the twentieth century involved dosing patients into stupor with barbiturates and keeping them unconscious for several days in the hope that this process would restore them to a desired state of mental health. Physicians then discovered that in certain cases depressed patients who experienced epileptic fits had less severe symptoms of mental illness. By causing a person to have a controlled fit (first by dosing them with camphor, then, from 1938, by the use of electricity), practitioners claimed they could lessen the effects of depression. Electro-convulsive therapy (ECT) remains to this day a highly contentious method of treatment, but is still employed in cases of severe depression by a dwindling number of advocates. It is difficult to read the material coming from patients and medical historians (e.g. Whitaker, 2002) without coming to the overwhelming conclusion that ECT, however packaged, prettified and rationalized, is a distinctly primitive form of experimentation, with often crippling consequences for those who have been subjected to it.

The beginnings of modern treatments

But we were bound to continue our mining of the brain and consensus grew that an understanding of depression depended on an understanding of the brain itself. This took a leap in 1928, when Austrian scientist Otto Loewi discovered the first neurotransmitter in the brain, acetylcholine. He concluded that this substance was necessary to help tiny electrical messages pass through the brain, from one nerve ending (neuron) to the next. Not until the 1950s would scientists discover the presence of noradrenaline, dopamine and serotonin, other neurotransmitter substances in the brain. During subsequent decades research proliferated and by the 1980s scientists had isolated 40 different neurotransmitter substances in the brain.

Advances in the understanding of brain chemistry ran simultaneously with the waning popularity of psychoanalysis. The unpopularity of medical practices like ECT and lobotomy (surgical removal of the frontal lobes of the brain) seemed to colour the whole profession. The popular image emerged of the psychoanalyst as a sex-obsessed fanatic who had the power to pronounce people insane and confine them to hospitals. Among analysts themselves, Freud's ideas began to be seen as old-fashioned and often inappropriate to modern needs. I recall some graffiti behind Freud's statue in London, back in the 1980s: 'My insights have spawned a monstrous repression'. As more drugs became available, psychoanalysis was seen as time-consuming, costly and with unreliable results.

The poet Philip Larkin famously wrote that sexual intercourse was invented in 1963 between the Lady Chatterley verdict and the Beatles' first LP. There is likewise a sense among many medical historians that depression, along with the proliferation of other forms of mental conditions as we know them in the twenty-first century, was invented in the 1950s. Two drug breakthroughs occurred in this decade. First, Roland Kuhn and Nathan Kline respectively discovered the drugs imipramine, and iproniazid, an anti-tuberculosis drug. Imipramine, when given to people who also had schizophrenia, made them more agitated. Depressed people who took the drug became more sociable, and interest in their surroundings returned, as did their appetites. Imipramine is still available today as Tofranil. It was the first tricyclic antidepressant medication (the term 'tricyclic' refers to the drug's atomic structure).

This was also the decade when American scientists began to examine whether levels of serotonin dropped when people were experiencing mental illness. This work led, in 1960, to the suggestion by English scientists that when a person was depressed the levels of serotonin in their blood fell dramatically.

A second type of antidepressant was also developed in the 1950s, known as monoamine oxidase inhibitors (MAOI). Like tricyclics, these are still available today, under brand names such as Nardil, Parnate and Mannerix. They work by blocking the action of certain substances in the brain (oxidases) which break down neurotransmitters, thus 'bathing' the brain in extra quantities of neurotransmitters. Though seen in medical circles as an effective remedy, these drugs can have an unpleasant or even fatal reaction when taken alongside certain foods and drink containing a substance called tyramine. The chief food to avoid is cheese, but the list includes avocado, banana, caviar, tinned figs, pickled herring, liver, smoked sausage, yeast extracts including Bovril, Marmite and Oxo, and broad bean pods, sometimes eaten when beans are young (Healy, 2002).

'Magic bullets'

Most early antidepressants worked by affecting several different neurotransmitter chemicals at the same time. But scientists began to work on drugs that would target one specific neurotransmitter while leaving others unaffected. For this reason they were named 'magic bullets'. In 1968 the Swedish scientist Arvid Carlsson made discoveries that would eventually lead to the creation of the drug fluoxetine, brand name Prozac. He found that when an electrical impulse passed from one neuron to another, the substance serotonin was released into the space between the neurons – the synapse – to help the 'message' transmit (see Figure 2, p. 50). After it had done its job, the serotonin was reabsorbed by the neuron. But antidepressant intake prevented the neurons from taking the serotonin back. The serotonin remained in the synapse, where its presence seemed to help the patient feel relief. Carlsson went on to make the first selective serotonin reuptake inhibitor (SSRI) – zimelidine.

Some years later, in 1974, American scientists were testing a drug which prevented the neurons from reabsorbing serotonin, while not preventing the absorption of other brain chemicals, such as noradrenaline. Its name was fluoxetine. In tests, they discovered that it was weakly and unreliably antidepressant. By 1987, the drug was being prescribed to patients as Prozac. By 1994, it was the number two best-selling drug in the world.

Despite widespread media and marketing frenzies, Prozac and its younger sisters have not been the 'wonder drugs' they were first hyped to be. It is now clear that SSRIs can lead to significant physical dependence (Glenmullen, 2005). There have been reports recently that they may be the main causative factor in suicidal thoughts and violence in certain individuals. Both the UK Medical and Healthcare products Regulatory Agency (MHRA) and the US Food and Drug Administration (FDA) have issued warnings regarding the dangers of these drugs.

Robert Whitaker, a notable critic of the medicalization of mental illness, observed:

A century ago, fewer than two people in 1,000 were considered to be 'disabled' by mental illness and in need of hospitalization. By 1955 that number had jumped to 3.38 people per 1,000, and during the past 50 years, a period when psychiatric drugs have been the cornerstone of care, the disability rate has climbed steadily, and has now reached around 20 people per 1,000 [in need of hospitalization]. As with any epidemic, one would suspect that an outside agent of some type – a virus, a bacterial infection, or an environmental toxin was causing this rise in illness. That is indeed the case here ... it is to be found in the medicine cabinet. Psychiatric drugs perturb normal neurotransmitter function, and while that perturbation may curb symptoms over a short term, over the long run it increases the likelihood that a person will become chronically ill, or ill with new and more severe symptoms. A review of the scientific literature shows quite clearly that it is our drug-based paradigm of care that is fuelling this modern-day plague.

(Whitaker, 2002)

Other remedies

Other drug remedies for depression continue to be developed (see Table 4.1, p. 55). Two additions were venlafaxine, which targets both serotonin and noradrenaline, and reboxetine, which targets noradrenaline.

Since the 1960s, herbal and homeopathic remedies have also become popular; particularly, impressive claims have been made for the quality and effectiveness of St John's Wort (hypericum). Cognitive behavioural therapy is also being used increasingly for people with depression, often alongside medication. Cognitive behavioural psychotherapy concentrates not on past experiences but on alerting us to negative and destructive patterns of thought, and on providing us with alternative, 'positive' models of thinking (see Chapter 6).

Current history

To this day no single agreed explanation for the biological, chemical or experiential causes of depression exists; we still do not know the nature of depression or its boundaries. For instance, though many of the remedies prescribed work immediately to increase the availability of neurotransmitters in the brain, it is usually two to six weeks before the patient reports an improvement in mood, sometimes longer and sometimes not at all. So to say that 'more neurotransmitters equals less depression' is inaccurate. Scientific interest has moved away from the neurotransmitter substances themselves and on to the mechanisms which allow them to be absorbed – and these have been found to be much more complex than first imagined. Other studies are examining the body's response to stress; it has been suggested that people who experience depression produce abnormally large amounts of the hormone cortisol when they are under stress.

However, mainstream psychiatry is no longer as deeply divided as it once was. At present most healthcare professionals are unable to provide sufficient counselling and psychotherapy; access to these services tends to be for the privileged few. It is increasingly agreed that medication when deemed necessary should be cautiously administered, and when considered necessary, best accompanied by counselling.

Psychiatry was once criticized for 'boundary violations', where physicians exploited the dependence of patients. Current indications are that psychiatry is in a new era of boundary violations, this time drug-related, most obviously in the case of depression and bipolar disorder, with adults treated with bizarre cocktails and children put on some of the most lethal drugs at our disposal (see Appendix 3). It is also a fact that one person's cure may be another's poison. David Healy observes:

> My first awareness of this [how individuals vary in response to drug treatments] came from a very simple practical exercise, almost 30 years ago in medical school. A group of 10 of us were given a beta-blocker to take. This should slow the heart rate, and it did – for nine of us – but one of the group had a marked increase in heart rate. This suggested that she was 'wired up' differently to the rest of us. A few years later the lesson was brought home again in a study giving clonidine to some colleagues. Clonidine lowers the concentration of noradrenaline in the bloodstream, and in the group as a whole it clearly did so, but in 20% of those investigated it produced an increase. (Healy, 2002)

In other words, one-size-fits-all dosages and blanket prescribing constitute very blunt instruments rather than the acclaimed 'magic bullet'.

Since at least 2002, experts concerned about over-medicating patients have been grappling with the notion, particularly in the United States where prescription drugs are openly advertised, that medicine has been derailed from its rightful mission of treating mental and other illness and is expanding under the influence of marketing strategies to engage in 'disease-mongering'. Viewed by many as legalized drug-pushing in the name of preventive medicine, disease-mongering can turn healthy people into patients, waste

Just another black dog day . . .

precious resources and even cause iatrogenic (medically induced) harm. Like the marketing strategies that drive it, disease-mongering poses a global challenge to the integrity of our healthcare systems, according to the Public Library of Science.

Yet depression remains the biggest social problem in the UK, and Richard Layard, emeritus professor at the London School of Economics, has claimed that around 15 per cent of the population suffers from depression or anxiety. He notes that the economic cost in terms of lost productivity is huge – around £17 billion, or 1.5 per cent of the UK's gross domestic product. He estimates that there are more than 1 million mentally ill people receiving incapacity benefit – more than the total number of unemployed people receiving unemployment benefit.

In addition, the National Institute for Clinical Excellence (NICE) advises that drugs are not the best answer. Richard Layard states that around 800,000 patients a year would require cognitive behavioural therapy. That means the country needs an extra 10,000 therapists – music to the ears of many a psychotherapist!

Since the focus in mental health for the last several decades has been on drugs alone, there have been no controlled studies documenting the effectiveness of psychotherapy and the effect of a sympathetic listener. Here is an open question: if it is true that an incompetent therapist can do great harm, which is the lesser harm – the bad therapy, or drugs whose hazardous effects are now well documented? David Healy observes: 'I know some therapists who've done tons of harm and few who do much good.' If he is correct, it appears that the professional treatment of depression remains a risky business whatever we choose.

3

The black dog and the spectre of suicide

Suicide is an act of violence against that part of ourselves that wants to go on living.

(Dorothy Rowe)

Suicidal thoughts are not recognized as a central component of depression, although common sense tells us that depression can lead to suicidal impulses, and there is an obvious link between suicide and emotional distress. A rough estimate from the Office for National Statistics (2004) indicates that a quarter of those who kill themselves each year in the UK will have been in contact with mental health services in the previous year.

I am a survivor of my daughter's suicide. Following her death the doctor diagnosed my grief as depression and for a while I accepted medication, but ceased taking the tablets when the side effects proved too debilitating. Although I believe I know what caused Caitlin to kill herself, and that she did not suffer from undiagnosed depression, I cannot prove this. The hard fact is that the truth of suicide (most often) dies with people who kill themselves, and remains a mystery still to be unravelled. The word 'mystery' comes from the Greek *myein*, which is used for the closing of the petals of a flower as well as of the eyelids. A natural movement of concealment and protection. Survivors of the terrible mystery of suicide must somehow pick up the pieces of our lives; we will inevitably for a time try to find answers to the 'why' of our loved one's self-execution.

Cultural and historical research reveals variations in attitude towards suicide in different times and countries. We learn of suicides in crowds, of dervish-like dancers in medieval central Europe, of Russian villagers running into the flames, of young women flinging themselves into a volcano in twentieth-century Japan. We learn of plunges from lover's leaps, special bridges, churches, monuments and towers. Entire communities, sects and corporations have fallen on the sword to the last breathing person rather than surrender.

Then there are the Christian martyrs. I quote John Donne on the certainty that martyrdom meant a clear way to heaven: 'many were baptized only because they would be burnt'. Samson cried out, 'Let me die with the Philistines', as he pulled down the temple upon himself and his enemies. Oh dear. Was Samson a biblical version of a suicide bomber? And what of Judas Iscariot, called 'the first modern man' after hanging himself in despair at his betrayal of Christ?

History abounds with examples of 'noble' suicide – Petronius, the perfect Epicurean, opening and closing his veins at pleasure, exchanging gossip with his friends as he let out his blood for the last time. Or Seneca and Socrates, out of favour and their own executioners. Hero in the Hellespont, Sappho from the rock at Neritos, Cleopatra, Jocasta the wife-mother of Oedipus, Portia who would follow Brutus. Skipping roughly to modern times, what of Hart Crane, Thomas Beddoes, Cesare Pavese, Virginia Woolf, Condorcet, Castlereagh, Forrestal, Vargas, Hemingway, a daughter of Karl Marx, a son of Eugene O'Neill, of Thomas Mann, Robert Frost, Herman Melville?

Suicide ceased to be a criminal offence in the UK in 1961. Although statistics vary according to source, since that time the number of suicides in developed countries has generally increased at an exponential rate. Some would argue that removal of the opprobrium once attached to suicide has made this final decision easier to take, most particularly in the case of young people who may be prone to reckless behaviours and decisions taken on the spur of the moment; our drug culture has undoubtedly made matters even more difficult.

Quantifying the risk of suicide

The Pierce Suicide Intent Score Scale (Pierce, 1981) is widely used as an attempt to quantify the risk of suicidality in patients. It is considered a useful tool in suicide risk assessment, but not as useful in clinical practice. However, for the many of us who have suffered depressive episodes, who have had suicidal thoughts at any time, the scale is an interesting indicator of survivor intentions. Remember: this test is given to people who have lived through an attempt on their own lives.

Circumstances related to a suicide attempt

1 Isolation

Somebody present	0
Somebody nearby or in contact	1
No one nearby or in contact	2

2 Timing

Timed so that intervention is probable	0
Timed so that intervention is not likely	1
Timed so that intervention is highly unlikely	2

3 Precautions against discovery

No precautions	0
Passive precautions, e.g. avoiding others but doing nothing to prevent intervention (e.g. alone in room, door unlocked)	1
Active precautions such as locking doors	2

4 Acting to gain help during or after attempt

Notified potential helper regarding attempt	0
Contacted but did not specifically notify potential helper regarding attempt	1
Did not contact or notify potential helper	2

5 Final acts in anticipation of death

None	0
Partial preparation or obsessive thinking	1
Definite plans made (e.g. changes in will, insurance)	2

6 Suicide note

Absence of note	0
Note written but torn up	1
Presence of note	2

Self report

1 *Statement of lethality*
Thought what s/he had done would not kill her/him   0
Unsure if what s/he had done would be lethal   1
Believes what s/he did would be lethal   2

2 *Stated intent*
Did not want to die   0
Uncertain or didn't care if s/he lived or died   1
Did want to die   2

3 *Premeditation*
Impulsive, no premeditation   0
Considered act for less than one hour   1
Considered act for less than one day   2
Considered act for more than one day   3

4 *Reaction to the act*
Patient glad s/he recovered   0
Patient uncertain whether glad or sorry   1
Patient sorry s/he has recovered   2

Risk

1 *Predictable outcome in terms of lethality of patient's act and*
circumstances known to him/her
Survival certain   0
Death unlikely   1
Death likely or certain   2

2 *Would death have occurred without medical treatment?*
No   0
Uncertain   1
Yes   2

Suicide intent score
Low: 0–3
Moderate: 4–10
High: over 11

Bereavement by suicide

(Portions of the following section were first published in my book *Losing a Child: Explorations in Grief*, and in *Spiritual and Ethical Issues of Suicide: Proceedings of the tenth annual conference*, Irish Association of Suicidology, Armagh, 2005.)

My normal and undepressed daughter was two months short of her twentieth birthday when she died. Her descent to suicide began innocently. After a visit to a relative's home in the USA, she said she'd seen an advert on television for a pill called Prozac, promising positive feelings and happiness. When she asked her relative about the drug he said it was a modern miracle, that she'd feel great and as a bonus probably lose weight too. So on return home, despite my mild and uninformed warnings that there's no such thing as a magic pill, she went to our GP and was prescribed it. A few weeks later and following a continuing descent into previously unthinkable chaos, my partner found Caitlin hanging from a beam in our guest bedroom.

When anyone of any age, depressed or not, dies by self-execution, all measurement becomes meaningless to those who loved this person. Bereavement by suicide holds much in common with

sudden death by any cause, although reactions are likely to be more intense and long-lasting. There is no chance for farewells, and when the death is violent there is an added legacy of shock shared with relatives of sudden death by accident and with murder victims. The unique factor in suicide is having to live with the truth that the death was self-inflicted execution, and may have been deliberately chosen. Survivors are devastated by the thought that we could not rescue our loved one, who must have suffered a despair so intense that it led to self-annihilation. Is this survivor state a kind of depression? I think not, although undoubtedly depression can attend the bereaved state.

How common is suicide?

At a conservative estimate there are 24,000 cases of attempted suicide by adolescents (of 10–19 years) each year in England and Wales, which is one attempt every 20 minutes. The statistics are much higher in Northern Ireland, where the young male population is affected the most. Depression is stated as a quantified risk factor, among many others, including being female. For example, those born in India and East Africa have a 40 per cent higher suicide rate than those born in England and Wales (NHS Framework for Mental Health). Hopelessness is unsurprisingly an important factor.

The following are some figures from the Office of National Statistics for England and Wales. Every year some 5,000 people kill themselves in England and Wales. Some 200,000 people, that we know of, attempt suicide each year, although the true number is likely to be much higher. In the age group 15–19, nearly 800 people in 100,000 try to kill themselves – this is double the number that did so ten years ago. Young people are at highest risk of suicide, and clumsily labelled 'completed' or 'successful' (as in 'she successfully completed a degree in suicide?') suicides are increasing more rapidly in this group than any other, and is the third most common cause of death for young people. People who have tried to kill themselves previously are more than 1,000 times as likely to try again than someone who has not.

Whether we are depressed or not, thinking about suicide is not uncommon; it is not simply the province of the severely depressed

or mentally unstable – a permanent solution to a temporary problem – in our culture. We don't like to say how often it is thought
about, not least because we fear that if we speak about it we may
contribute to an epidemic.

Self-destruction once carried powerful disincentives – if the
prospect of hell did not put off the would-be suicide, the fear
of prison might; of course, the fear of prison could also make
those vulnerable to suicide more determined to 'get it right' too.
Nonetheless, suicide has undergone a rapid rehabilitation. The
crime of the 1950s has become, in the euthanasia debate of the
1990s and early 2000s, an action affiliated to personal dignity.
Suicide has become more acceptable.

A benign concept of death, a loosening of moral prohibitions and
an emphasis on personal freedom have combined to create relatively
liberal attitudes. It is possible that greater tolerance has reduced
the number of psychological obstacles standing between young
people and suicide. There is also some evidence that liberal and
secular morals may encourage acceptance of euthanasia and suicide
as an aspect of individual rights. For example, European countries
suffering the sharpest drop in church membership in the 1960s and
mid-1980s suffered sharper increases in youth suicide (Hill, 1995).

The majority of suicides appear to involve either street drugs,
overdoses of alcohol or medication or adverse/toxic reactions
to medications. All of these substances can increase states of
depression, anxiety and altered thought patterns. The alarming rise
in numbers of suicides of our children, and in mental disability
in general, runs in tandem with the appearance (since 1990) of
medications targeted to treat a variety of conditions common to
young people, and it is fair to observe that (a) a good proportion
of those who died were taking medication to treat one or more of
these conditions, and (b) death by suicide is not supposed to be
what happens when a medication works.

Sex and social pressures

Relationship difficulties are often implicated in young suicide
attempts – in one study, over half (52 per cent) of adolescents
who took an overdose reported having problems with a boyfriend

or girlfriend. The underlying causes of unhappiness are likely to be more profound than this, but vulnerable young people, and indeed people of all ages, clearly experience acute stress when their relationships go wrong. Sexual intimacy raises the emotional stakes exponentially, and makes rejection much worse.

Changes attending attitudes to suicide are also true of attitudes to sex. Earlier sexual activity has exposed young people to the emotional and physical risks of sex as well as its pleasures. The sexual revolution of the 1960s separated sex from the necessity of marriage and the fear of conception. Premarital sex became more common and young people began sexual relationships at an earlier age. The 'guesstimate' average age for sexual intercourse in girls is now said to be 15 (I conducted a straw poll by asking 20 of Caitlin's sixth-form friends, male and female, when they became 'non-virgins', which produced the same average age of 15). One young man recalled that 'At around 14 or 15 there is all this emphasis on "shagging". It's expected that you really wanted to "do it".' This isn't to say that casual sex is the norm, but neither are long-term involvements. Much more normally, teens have intense short-term relationships which will, again normally, cause pain when they end.

Our family has certainly had personal experience of the pressures I'm talking about. After a difficult separation and divorce, I moved from my clergy husband's vicarage to a small rural community with Caitlin and my partner Trish. Caitlin's older brother Sean was by now living independently in London. Caitlin made friends quickly and easily. She loved living in the country and visiting her father regularly in London. However, not long into her first term at the local school she came home crying.

'Darling, what's wrong?'

'They laughed at me in science today, Mum.'

'Why?'

'One of the boys shouted out in front of everybody, "Hey Caitlin, do you do threesomes with your mum?" And everybody just laughed at me. The teacher didn't do anything except tell everyone to settle down – she seemed to think it was funny too.'

Then she said, 'Mum, what's a threesome?'

I tried to explain what I understand to be a threesome. I was cut to the heart on her behalf. She was happy for me to see her teacher and the principal of the school to sort things out. The school responded quickly and skilfully, and that, I thought, was that. Except it wasn't. It turned out that even at the ages of 13 and 14, Caitlin was being challenged by her peers. 'C'mon, prove you're not a lezzie', was the gist. Caitlin wasn't singled out in this way; her girlfriends from traditional nuclear families and solo parent homes too got similar taunting.

We signed up for family counselling so that we could, for want of a better term, normalize our new life together as Trish and I tried to find out how to be better parents to Caitlin in a non-traditional family setting in a community where there are quite simply no secrets. Since our family unit was 'unusual', i.e. consisting of two 'mums', we recognized prejudices which might be unfairly directed at Caitlin. We also wanted Caitlin to be reassured that she was a normal young girl. She had her own personal counsellor throughout, and the report at the end of the sessions described Caitlin as a healthy, confident, balanced and positive girl whose developing sexuality was entirely normal. We found the counsellors affirming and very helpful.

Pressure on Caitlin and her friends from her male peer group to be sexually active continued. This, I learned later, is characteristic of a crude attitude in our area that 'If there's grass on the pitch the game's on', especially when the girl concerned is very pretty, as Caitlin and her friends were. How widespread the attitude is, I don't know, but this pressure, unsavoury as it is, was echoed by her older brother's girlfriend of the time. Then in her early twenties, she said that Caitlin should have as much sex and with as many boys as she could. I was furious but helpless. Nobody asked Caitlin what *she* wanted, and quite naturally she was listening more to her peers than to me or my partner. When I tried to discuss my concerns with Caitlin her response was typical of her: 'Oh Mum, don't be such a prude-y moody Trudy!'

Caitlin was an optimist; she wanted to be a lawyer and a singer and a movie star, simultaneously. After that brief patch of bullying in middle school, she stood up for herself, as did her friends and teachers, and mum and partner too, and came out the other side stronger and more capable. She grew up believing that teachers and electricians and doctors and gardeners and lawyers, plumbers and politicians are mainly pretty good people. We talked about this – people on the whole, we agreed, prefer the buzz of helping others feel better to the buzz of doing mischief. Those who didn't come from our 'take' on life were the type of 'saddo' who appeared on Oprah and Ricki Lake and Jerry Springer, on talk shows and in shocking television documentaries and tabloids – the *not-us* people; and though I was a far from perfect parent, she always let me know that 'You're always *there* for me, Mum.'

On being the survivor

The desperation of suicide, as well as the depressive state that can sometimes trigger the act, is well documented. Many contend that suicide is an aggressive act, the ultimate revenge. Sometimes suicide can indeed be hatred, turned against oneself, but inflicting a wound that cannot be healed or redressed by those who live on. Dr Edwin Schneidman, author of numerous books on suicide, wrote:

> I believe that the person who commits suicide puts his psycho-
> logical skeleton in the survivor's emotional closet – he sentences
> the survivor to deal with many negative feelings and, more,
> to become obsessed with thoughts regarding his own actual or
> possible role in having precipitated the suicidal act or having
> failed to abort it.

Guilt is often a large component of depression, sadness and grief, and it is extremely difficult to avoid feeling guilty when a person we love ends their life, that to some degree we were responsible. Why didn't I ring back? Why did I get so angry? Why didn't I stay with her instead of going to work? Why did I let him go off that weekend in the middle of an argument? And what if we find out we *were* responsible? What if they write a last vengeful letter saying it was our fault? Most unfortunately, they are not around to debate the other predisposing factors in the parts of their life that did not include us. The only appropriate arena for guilt is if we set our loved one up to die by suicide. And, hard as it sounds, the 'if onlys' of the past also aren't going to help any of us.

Even for families who have lived for years with a loved one's emotional problems, their repeated attempts at self-destruction and inability to believe that the future might be better, the actual death is still a profound shock. More often, there is no such introduction; the suicide comes out of the blue, and the police are at the door telling me something I cannot begin to absorb.

In spite of my observations about the difficult aspects of recent shifts in societal attitudes, clearly I am thankful that suicide is not regarded any more as a criminal or sinful act. Within families, reactions to this tragedy will be diverse, and differences can be very divisive. Misunderstandings can grow as each grieving person pursues a disparate road. Rifts can widen and real estrangement can occur, even between partners who thought ourselves previously close. Marriages and partnerships become extremely vulnerable. They can and do break down in the aftermath of the death of a child for any reason; suicidal deaths compound the dangers. My life partner has left our home during the writing of this book, for reasons directly related to my personal problems of depression and grief as a mother following Caitlin's death and in spite of stupendous efforts on both our parts to understand the different ways that we grieve and survive.

A good example of being 'marked' by judgement from others after suicide by a family member was a comment from a parent of one of Caitlin's college friends. Trish and I founded a scholarship in Caitlin's memory, now a registered charity called Caitlin's Kickstart Award, to benefit students from our rural community having difficulty in continuing formal studies as a result of the government's change from the grant system to a loan system for higher education. The comment was, 'Don't you think you are in danger of glorifying your daughter's suicide by doing this?' I responded with gape-mouthed silence, but wish I'd reminded her that there were many times, like futile wars, where we fear our children may have sacrificed their lives in vain, but that this does not make it a bad idea to remember and honour the lives they lived, no matter how brief and imperfect. And, of course, to do something positive in the wake of tragedy which will help others.

Caitlin's death and the involvement of toxicity in the medication she was taking, also revealed the flip side of a rosy dream – a realization that behind the institutions and professions born of and based on humanitarian principles lurks a less benevolent mammal, capable of misusing power, bent on profit for its own sake. Soon after her death, at the inquest to be exact, I heard solid evidence that Caitlin had only one substance in her body at the time of her death: a therapeutic dose of fluoxetine hydrochloride (Prozac), her prescription medication.

Loved ones bereaved by suicide can deal with 'hows' if we can investigate the 'whys', leaving no stone unturned. The trail doesn't always lead anywhere. We may never discover the answer, but I would not discourage anyone from going down the 'why' road – with this caveat: knowing why changes nothing – our loved one is dead and will not come back on this earth, and in that sense our search is not 'helpful'. But if cases like Caitlin's can be understood and acted on, lives will be saved.

Caitlin wanted Prozac because she believed an ad she saw on holiday in America, where the advertising of medications is legal. She believed what 'everyone' else was saying about it – its celebrity endorsements, its much-lauded feel-good factor and slimming properties as much as anything; all she had to do was say the right words to her well-meaning doctor. It took her seven minutes to do so.

Forgiveness as an antidote to depression

To my mind one of the best true tales of modern forgiveness comes from Enniskillen in Northern Ireland. It is Sunday 8 November 1987, Remembrance Sunday. Gordon Wilson and his daughter Marie, a young nurse, arrive at the Cenotaph to remember the dead. An IRA bomb explodes. Gordon and Marie take a direct hit from the blast. Gordon survives his serious injuries but Marie dies. The following morning Gordon is interviewed on a news report:

> The wall collapsed ... and we were thrown forward ... rubble and stones ... all around us and under us. I remember thinking ... 'I'm not hurt' ... but there's a pain in my shoulder ... I shouted to Marie, 'Are you all right?' and she said, 'Yes' ... She found my hand and said, 'Is that your hand, Dad?' ... I said, 'Are you all right, dear?' ... but we were under six feet of rubble ... three or four times I asked her ... she always said, 'Yes, I'm all right' ... I asked her the fifth time ... 'Are you all right, Marie?' ... She said,

'Daddy, I love you very much'. Those were the last words she spoke to me ... I kept shouting, 'Marie, are you all right?' ... There was no reply. I have lost my daughter, but I bear no ill will, I bear no grudge ... Dirty sort of talk is not going to bring her back to life ... I don't have an answer ... But I know there has to be a plan. If I didn't think that, I would commit suicide ... It's part of a greater plan, and God is good ... And we shall meet again.

In a few broken sentences, Gordon Wilson's words entered the collective memories of millions. He spent the years following Enniskillen working in his quiet way for the elimination of hatred and misunderstanding. If only we could bottle the gift of a Gordon Wilson!

Using depression to heal

Time to reflect has brought to me a new cell of an idea: what if, in cases where suicide *is* revenge – against self first and foremost, but against friends, family, society, whatever – we could find a way to transform the rage and revenge and extinguished mechanisms of reality into something life-affirming?

Dorothy Rowe, lauded in *Saga* magazine as one of the 50 wisest women in the world and certainly one of my favourite human beings on the planet, claims, through decades of counselling depressed people, that 95 per cent of what happens to us is determined by the ideas we hold about the conditions of our lives.

So many of us who have had suicidal thoughts are perfectionists who've been brought up to expect a great deal from life and who have been thwarted in our desire to give it back. Sometimes we make unrealistic demands on ourselves, wanting more than is possible to obtain. A different set of rules seems to operate, often exacerbated by the models of perfection constantly bombarding from all directions.

(Rowe, 2001)

There are active organizations dedicated to preventing suicide and helping survivors. UK-based PAPYRUS produces leaflets and holds conferences as well as participating in the government's working paper on suicide prevention. The Irish Association of Suicidology was founded in 1996. Among its aims and objectives are:

- to facilitate communication between clinicians, volunteers, survivors and researchers in all matters relating to suicide and suicidal behaviour;
- to promote awareness of the problems of suicide and suicidal behaviour in the general public by holding conferences and workshops and by communication of relevant material through the media;
- to ensure that the public is better informed about suicide prevention;
- to support and encourage relevant research;
- to encourage and support the formation of groups to help those bereaved by suicide.

There are talking therapies and programmes, and videos, unfortunately not yet widely available. TCF (The Compassionate Friends) on whose national committee I served as trustee, is a befriending organization for bereaved families, with a national helpline and special contact group for survivors of suicide.

There are warning signs of suicidal thinking. Some of these are:

- Talking about it. The common wisdom is that talking about suicide is the equivalent to 'crying wolf'. Not true.
- Sudden changes in behaviour, being either withdrawn or 'speedy', disruptive, or violent.
- Taking unnecessary risks.
- Increased alcohol or drug intake, both illegal and/or prescribed.
- Changes in eating habits.
- 'Bunking off' school or work; decline in work quality.
- Ending of a relationship.
- Bereavement (can be very vulnerable if the death was by suicide).
- Self-harming.
- Despondency and loss of interest in life. Depression.
- Adverse reactions to medication, including intense agitation (akathisia), nightmares, emotional blunting, self-harm.

Suicide survivors may be able to help others. For one thing we can disabuse people of certain kinds of misinformation, for example the notion that those who think suicide is just an easy way out for cowards need to know that suicidal thoughts are not a respecter of persons. The reality is that all kinds of normal people, including, and sometimes particularly, those who appear to be strong, are vulnerable to killing themselves. Those people, including the more sympathetic among us, who think that hushing up about suicide when we're worried about a loved one's behaviour is the best plan, should think again. Listening to/talking to a trusted someone about suicidal despair can be life-saving.

Here are some of the more common misunderstandings about suicide (with thanks to Dr Howard Rosenthal for a version of this list).

- *Suicidal people don't give warning signs.* Not true. Nearly everyone who attempts or commits suicide communicates the intention. She or he may joke about it, go to internet chatrooms, write about it, draw visuals related to death by suicide. Giving away prized possessions can be a warning too.
- *Suicide occurs around the holidays.* In fact in the UK December and the New Year are lower suicide times, as are other major holiday times.
- *The danger of suicide is greater in wintertime.* Most suicides actually occur in April and May.
- *Suicide is mainly a young person's problem.* The rate of teen suicides has trebled since the 1960s. The rate in women rises until it peaks in the early fifties and then plateaus. The suicide rate of young men in Northern Ireland has seen an alarming rise in recent years; in the general male population, suicide rates continue to increase with age, with the rate of geriatric suicide (age 65 and older) running at approximately three times the general population.
- *Most people leave a note.* The estimate is that just 15 to 25 per cent of those who die by suicide leave a note.
- *People living in big cities are more vulnerable to suicide.* The suicide rate is in fact higher in rural and sparsely populated areas.
- *The state of the economy does not affect the suicide rate.* In troubled economic times, suicide rates skyrocket. An example would be during the Great Depression in the United States in 1929.
- *The grief of survivors of suicide is just like any other grief.* People who have lost a loved one to suicide have a tougher time coping with grief; one cannot blame a virus or a madman or a drunk driver.

- *During times of war the suicide rate rises.* Suicide rates plummet during wartimes.
- *Never ask a person if s/he is suicidal, as you might put the idea in their head.* No! Make a point of asking your sad and depressed friend if s/he is feeling suicidal.
- *When depression lifts, the danger has passed.* In reality the lifting of the depressive state can be the most vulnerable and dangerous time.
- *Don't bother giving your suicidal friend the number of the Samaritans if s/he insists the call won't be made.* The truth is that many people who say they would never ring a hotline will decide to make the call. Like the rest of us, suicidal folk may change their minds.

If someone tells you she or he is thinking about suicide, there are some things you can say:

> 'The problem is awful, I know, but it is temporary and you can get help to solve it. But your solution is permanent.'
> 'You are suffering so much. Your suffering can be alleviated and you can get better.'
> 'Is there anything to lose if you seek some help?'
> 'If you choose to die at your own hands, this action will permanently harm your family and loved ones.'

(The last example in the list above is *not* a guilt trip. People in the fugue-like tunnel of suicidal ideation are often not thinking of others. Of course, if the person contemplating self-killing is feeling vengeful, this suggestion won't stop them.)

If, as you read this book, you recognize danger signs in your life that have brought thoughts of suicide, please wait. Contact someone you can talk to. There will be a light at the end of the tunnel, and it will not be an oncoming train. Suicide is, as the truism goes, a permanent solution to a temporary problem. Turn to your most trusted friend and seek to find the part of you that loves this life, wants to live. If the friend is on answerphone, leave a message and wait until they reach you to talk. Choose life. Please.

4

The disease model of depression

Not much is understood about the biochemistry of depression and its treatment, except in general terms ... This suggests that the therapeutic action of antidepressants is not to cure the depression itself but to hold the symptoms in check until the illness lifts of its own accord.

(Malcolm Lader, Professor of Pharmacology, Institute of Psychiatry, London, quoted in Dorothy Rowe, *Depression: The Way Out of Your Prison*, p. 181)

Unlike other consumer products, medicine is a two-edged sword – its beneficial side depends on the integrity of the profession and the regulatory system. Medicine without integrity is a lethal weapon.

(Vera Hassner Sharav, Alliance for Human Research Protection)

I am a Bear of Very Little Brain, and long words bother me.

(A. A. Milne, *Winnie-the-Pooh*)

The venerated notion enshrined in the Declaration of Independence, that 'all men are created equal', doesn't hold much water in the world of human biology. Life is unfair. At conception the random association of genes encodes us human animals for biological characteristics, including diseases. People may be crippled by the simple process of being birthed. Some people have more wealth, position, intelligence, courage, stamina, strength, speed and coordination. None of us escapes wounding by family, friend and foe. However, genetics and circumstances (nature–nurture) are not absolute destiny. We can overcome. Move on. Make choices, plans and progress; life can be a beach as well as a bitch.

Our doctor diagnoses a physical illness, based on our history and symptoms, physical check-up, and information from laboratory tests. However, when depression is diagnosed, the criteria are subjective. There are at this time no medical tests that can accurately make a diagnosis of mental illness. This doesn't mean that such tests will never be available, but we don't have them yet. Statistics do not explain depression. Explanations must be sought in a multitude of disciplines: the social sciences, biological science, culture, anthropology, mythology, intuition, reflection and spirituality.

The structure of the brain

The brain is the major organ of our nervous system. It receives, sorts and interprets sensations from the nerves that extend from the central nervous system (made up of the brain and spinal cord), to the rest of the body. The brain initiates and coordinates nerve signals involved in speech, movement, thought and emotion. A mature brain weighs about 1.4 kg and consists of three main structures: the *cerebrum*, the largest part and consists of a left and a right hemisphere; the *brainstem*; and the *cerebellum*.

The cerebrum, which looks like a cauliflower, has an outer layer called the cortex, which consists of grey matter. Grey matter is rich in nerve cells and is the main region for conscious thought, sensation and movement. Beneath the grey matter of the cortex are tracts of nerve fibres called white matter, and deeper still within the hemispheres, the *basal ganglia*. The surface of each hemisphere is divided by fissures (*sulci*) and folds (*gyri*) into distinct lobes (occipital, frontal, parietal and temporal). These lobes are named after the skull bones that overlie them. A thick band of nerve fibres called the *corpus callosum* connects the hemispheres.

The cerebrum encloses a central group of structures that includes the *thalamus* and *hypothalamus*, which is closely connected to the pituitary gland. Encircling the thalamus is a complex of nerve centres called the *limbic system*. These structures act as links between parts of the cerebrum and the brainstem lying beneath the thalamus.

The brainstem is concerned mainly with the control of vital functions like breathing and blood pressure. The cerebellum at the back of the brain controls balance, posture and muscular coordination. Both of these regions operate at a subconscious level.

The brain and spinal cord are encased in three layers of membranes, known as *meninges*. Cerebrospinal fluid circulates between the layers and within the four main brain cavities called *ventricles*. This fluid helps to nourish and cushion the brain. About 20 per cent of the heart's output goes to the brain.

Brain structure and depression

The disease model of depression maintains that feelings of depression are most likely caused by chemical changes affecting how the brain functions. This is a logical assumption because a normally functioning brain is a giant messaging system controlling everything from our heartbeat, to walking, to our emotions. The brain is made up of millions of nerve cells called neurons. These neurons send and receive messages from the rest of our body, using chemicals called neurotransmitters. These brain chemicals are in varying amounts responsible for our emotional state. The assumption therefore contends that depression happens when these chemical messages aren't delivered correctly between brain cells, thus disrupting communication.

At the last count there were six overlapping sciences involved in depression research (Hunter, 2004): anatomy, neuropharmacology, genetics, endocrinology, engineering and epidemiology. One physician adds to this list serendipity, or happy accidents aided by clever application, claiming that serendipity has aided our understanding of how drugs affect the brain, and what happens to people when strokes or accidents 'insult' a part of the brain. We have been dissecting and studying the brain for centuries. Here is a layperson's breakdown of brain functions (see Figure 1, overleaf).

The *cerebrum* is the outer covering of most of the brain, and its outer layer, the cerebral cortex, is the grey matter. Within the cerebral cortex are the neurons or nerve cell bodies. Neurons are single-celled bodies and the basic functioning units of the brain. Beneath the grey matter is white matter, containing nerve fibres or *axons* which transmit messages between the neuron and other nerve centres in the central nervous system (brain and spinal cord). The cerebrum is in two halves, like a walnut, the right and left cerebral hemispheres. The left cerebral hemisphere controls the right side of the body, and the right cerebral hemisphere controls the left side. This is because most nerves cross from one side to another in the neck. Our five senses of touch, smell, hearing, taste and sight are 'interpreted' from areas of the cerebrum; it also programmes thought and facilitates the beginning of voluntary movement through muscle stimulation.

The *frontal lobes* exist on the front rim of the cerebrum. They control rationality, concentration, planning, envisioning the future, problem-solving and multi-tasking. This is the area of the brain that makes us unique as humans.

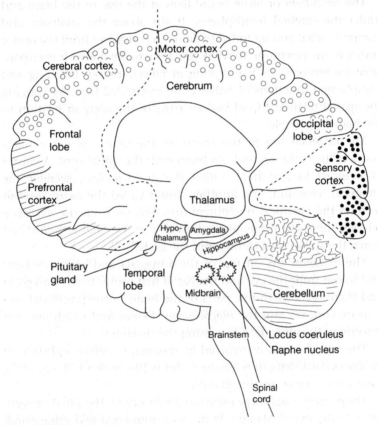

Figure 1 Brain bisection
This bisection shows the major functioning areas of the brain

The *sensory cortex* is located at the rear rim of the cerebral cortex. It receives sensory information from the *thalamus* and works in sympathy with the *prefrontal cortex* to interpret and act on stimuli. It helps distinguish real external threats from false alarms.

The *motor cortex* lies along both sides of the cerebrum and contains neurons which send signals to the muscles that control voluntary movement. Science has mapped which bits of the motor cortex control which muscles. The area controlling the human thumb is much larger than other motor areas, giving rise to the singularly human 'opposable thumb' which marks us out as tool makers and users.

The *cerebellum* or 'little brain' lives at the rear of the brain and under the cerebral hemispheres. It sits above the *midbrain*, and compares what you intended to do, i.e. a command from the motor cortex in the cerebrum, to what you are actually doing. It is responsible for motor skills like driving or bicycle riding. Learning and complicated functions of balance are controlled here, by gauging the spatial relationship of various parts of the body in relation to the body as a whole.

The *midbrain* lies in the centre of the brain; its nerve tracts connect the thalamus and cerebrum with the spinal cord. A cluster of neurons located here, called the *raphe nucleus*, secretes the chemical serotonin, and another cluster called the *locus coeruleus* secretes the chemical norepinephrine. Stimuli from the *amygdala* releases these chemicals to be dispersed to the 'higher brain' and down the spinal cord throughout the body.

The *thalamus* sits on top of the amygdala and processes sight and sound from the eye and the ear. It first routes to the amygdala and then to the cognitive parts of the brain in the prefrontal and sensory cortexes and the *hippocampus*. Odour and touch are sent directly to the amygdala, bypassing the thalamus.

The *hypothalamus* is involved in appetite, sex drive and sleep. It produces corticotropin releasing factor (CRF), which influences the function of our endocrine glands.

The *pituitary gland* is a pea-sized structure attached by a stalk of nerve fibres to the hypothalamus. As the most important endocrine gland, it is sometimes referred to as the 'master gland'. It secretes hormones which are critical to our endocrine system – adrenals, testes and ovaries, thyroid, parathyroid, and the pancreatic islets of Langerhans. The pituitary gland responds to CRF secreted by the hypothalamus to produce the adrenocorticotropic hormone ACTH, which influences the function of the endocrine glands.

The *amygdala* is central to brain function (its name is derived from the Latin for the shape of an almond), and it can be found at the base of the thalamus. Evolution describes the amygdala as the functioning brain of vipers and crocodiles; it is said to 'shoot first and ask questions later'. It produces primitive emotions like aggression, rage, fear, and basic life responses like licking and chewing. It is wired to react to threat, and does not wait for information from the frontal lobes of the cerebral cortex to sound an alarm. In virtually a nanosecond it charges the hypothalamus, the pituitary and the adrenal glands, and the body is flushed with cortisol, epinephrine and norepinephrine. As a result the heart thumps, the pulse races, the lungs inflate, the pupils widen, arteries expand and a surge of sugar enters the system. Simultaneously, non-essential body functions like stomach, bowel, kidneys, sex drive and immune systems close down – and sometimes bowel and bladder will involuntarily empty. Removing the amygdala in animals produces docility. Some scientists connect the functioning of the amygdala as playing a part in psychosis, mania and depression. It also helps form long-term memories affected by powerful emotions.

The *hippocampus*, after the Greek for 'seahorse', rests by the midbrain and the cerebellum and is located in the temporal lobes of the cerebrum. The hippocampus takes messages from the amygdala, integrates the sensory stimuli into the sensory and prefrontal cortices, and helps evaluate them in light of previous experiences. The hippocampus also functions in spatial orientation, constructing three-dimensional 'mental-maps' of the body in relation to where its 'place' is in its 'space'. Damage to the hippocampus, as with stroke survivors, makes it difficult for the person to navigate in what was once familiar territory. The hippocampus processes and stores short-term memories before transferring them to the cerebral cortex. Damage to the hippocampus makes it difficult to form new short-term memories.

The *limbic system*, a ring-shaped area in the centre of the brain, consists of a number of connected clusters of nerve cells. It plays a role

The brain labels: Cerebrum, Frontal lobe, Occipital lobe, Berserk lobe

THE BRAIN
Identifying the berserk

in influencing the autonomic nervous system which automatically regulates a number of body functions, the emotions, and the sense of smell. This extensive system contains various substructures which include the hippocampus, amygdala, hypothalamus and thalamus.

The *brainstem* gathers up all the nerve fibres streaming out of the cerebrum, cerebellum, thalamus and midbrain, and acts as a conduit connecting them to the spinal cord.

The *neuron* (see Figure 2, overleaf) is the term for a nerve cell, and was discovered using tools such as electron microscopes and by the joined forces of organic chemists, enzyme chemists and immunologists. From this teamwork was born cellular biology, whence emerged the identification of a single cell as the basic functioning unit of the brain. The nervous system contains billions of neurons, of which there are three main types: *sensory* neurons, which carry signals from sense receptors into the central nervous system; *motor* neurons, which carry signals from the central nervous system to muscles or glands; and *interneurons*, which form all the complex electrical circuitry within the central nervous system. The neuron has its own brain (nucleus), its own eyes and ears (short appendages called dendrites) and its own arm and hand (axon), which reaches out to neurons in other parts of the brain to transmit messages. Messages are passed by neurotransmitters. Neurons have dedicated tasks – sight, hearing, smell, touch, taste, motion, cognition, memory, balance, spatial perceptions, hormone production and the creation of emotions.

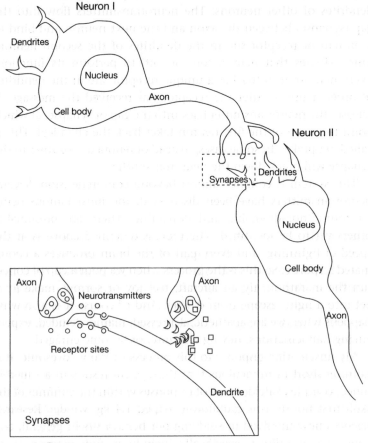

Figure 2 The neuron
A single cell – the basic functioning unit of the brain

The science of depression: singing the body electric

Neuropharmacology is the science of what chemicals affect brain function and how they do it. We have learned that a neuron communicates not by 'touching' another neuron but by crossing a gap or synapse between an axon and a neighbour neuron. Crossing the gap is the work of chemicals called neurotransmitters. Without these neurotransmitters the brain cannot function. When you stimulate a neuron an electric impulse passes down its arm and hand (axon); at the end of the axon are containers or vesicles filled with neurotransmitters which will be released by the electrical impulse. Each neurotransmitter has a unique receptor site in the dendrites of other neurons. The neurotransmitters flow into the gap (synapse) between the axon and the next neuron and bind to a protein or receptor site in the dendrites of the second neuron. This switches that neuron 'on' or 'off' to perform its function. Every neurotransmitter has a unique receptor site in the dendrites of other neurons. After the receptor has received the message, it releases the neurotransmitter back into the gap or synapse, at which point the axon of the first neuron takes back the chemical. This is called 'reuptake'. In some cases, instead of reuptake, enzymes in the synapse will break down the neurotransmitter.

This system is complex almost beyond comprehension. Several neurotransmitters have been discovered, the most famous being serotonin, noradrenaline and dopamine. There are presumably others yet to be identified. The process described above is at the speed of lightning, and every part of the brain produces a coordinated response. So this is the process when we pour a cup of coffee, run the marathon, fly an aircraft, feel joy or sorrow, make love, get into a fight, escape from danger. And of course it is also what happens when we are apathetic, depressed, manic, deluded, experiencing hallucinations, having a seizure, or become enraged.

My unscientific response to this process is: Wow. Awesome. It is nothing short of miraculous that this system results in a superbly tuned, complex kaleidoscope of responses within the confines of the skull that houses this cauliflower-shaped 1.4 kg wonder. Research sciences now involved in studying our behaviours in general, and depression as a disease specifically, include the following:

- *Genetics* The study of inheritance, the chemical basis by which characteristics are determined, and the causes of the similarities and differences among individuals of a species or between different species. Branches of genetics include population genetics, molecular genetics and clinical genetics. The latter is concerned with the study and prevention of genetic disorders.
- *Endocrinology* The study of the endocrine system. This system is the collection of glands around the body that produces hormones. These glands include the thyroid gland, pancreas, testes, ovaries and adrenal glands. These hormones are responsible for numerous bodily processes including growth, metabolism, sexual development and response to stress. Hormone secretion from many endocrine glands is regulated by the pituitary gland which is in turn influenced by the hypothalamus via a feedback system.
- *Epidemiology* The branch of medicine concerned with the occurrence and distribution of disease, including infectious diseases like influenza and non-infectious diseases like cancer. Members of a population are counted and described in terms of such variables as sex, race, age, class, occupation and marital status. In comparative epidemiological studies two or more groups become part of the study, for example to discover a link between the incidence of lung cancer in one group of smokers versus another group of non-smokers. The proportion of cancer in each group is then calculated.
- *Engineering* For our purposes the process of designing and building systems aimed at identifying and treating disease. In terms of researching depression, extensive efforts have been directed at trying to locate the birthplace of depression. *Positron emission tomography* (PET) has made possible pictures of brain anatomy and attempted to devise techniques which watch brain parts 'work'.

The PET scan

Images of the brain are taken in variations of blue, purple, yellow and orange colours. The picture that emerges shows various colours predominating in certain regions of the brain. Yellow and orange predominate when the person is not depressed. The colours relate to the use of sugar fuel in the brain cells. When more fuel is used the neurons are more active and produce the yellow and orange; when less fuel is used the neurons are less active and produce blue and purple.

The PET scan is, however, in one sense disappointing: so far it has revealed nothing beyond what a neurologist of the nineteenth century could have told us about brain functions and where they're localized. But extravagant claims continue to be made, despite the fact that the technique has not revealed anything new – other than providing a graphic depiction of the brain's surface activity. Hundreds of studies of these images are published in scientific journals each month as magnetic resonance imaging machines produce pictures with higher resolution. Benedict Carey wrote in the *New York Times*:

> If the hype is to be believed, neuroscientists will soon pinpoint the regions in the brain where mediocre poetry is generated, where high school grudges are lodged, where sarcasm blooms like a red rose. In the last month alone, researchers working with brain imaging machines have captured the neural trace of *schadenfreude* and the emotional flare of partisan thinking and whatever happens between the ears of a happily married woman when her husband takes her hand.

Lawyers have used brain imaging to help reduce criminal sentences, arguing that their clients' actions can partly be explained by the way their brains function, or malfunction. Some researchers say their imaging methods can help detect lies.

But what do these scans tell us about how we function, what motivates us, who we are? What are the hazards inherent in exaggerating the positives of what are, in fact, computer graphics? Neuroscientists debate these questions constantly, and even agree on some of the answers. It is beyond doubt that brain images reveal real biological activity associated with genuine human sensations, which is why people are so delighted and amazed to see images which show that there is a measurable physical response in the brain to their feelings. Moving away from the brain for a moment, if you are a parent and viewed a prenatal scan, recall your feelings when you saw that living being in the womb.

Understanding that the whole-body ache of longing leaves a physical trace in the brain seems to give people more sympathy for others' emotions and reactions, say neuroscientists who have presented findings in front of professional and lay audiences. The link to depression is this: think of a person who suffers from depression or bipolar disorder for whom nothing has helped. Scientists are hoping that there may be another way to treat the condition than treating it like a flaw in our character. There is a lot of optimism around.

The catch is that, for all their power, imaging machines are like the Mars probe: they see surfaces, mountain peaks, valleys – without being able to take samples of the underlying terrain. This is because the regions that peak in activity when a person is happy or guilty or jealous are connected to many other areas along complex circuits distributed throughout the brain that are, for the most part, still unlit by the computerized spotlight of the imaging machine. It is in these subterranean, subtle enfoldings of the brain, that neuroscientists say they are most likely to discover its deepest secrets.

Scientists also recognize a risk to the technology – that seeing the neural activity allows people to deny responsibility for their behaviour, in essence to compromise the individual person.

Medical treatment of depression

Medication has become the first port of call in our culture for the treatment of depression. Drugs that treat depression are called antidepressants. All these drugs (see Table 1) work by increasing the amount of neurotransmitters – serotonin, noradrenaline and dopamine – available to keep 'messages' moving between neurons. This happens in two ways: one is to prevent the neurotransmitters from being taken back into the axon of the neuron, i.e. blocking the 'reuptake' of the neurotransmitter. Thus the term 'reuptake inhibitor'. The second way the drugs work is by blocking the enzyme that breaks down the neurotransmitter. Since this enzyme is monoamine oxidase, these drugs are called monoamine oxidase inhibitors, or MAOIs. These drugs are decreasing in popularity, mainly because they can interfere with our metabolizing of certain foods, causing dangerous and even toxic side effects. These foods include cabbage, grapefruit, red wines, beer, beans and certain cheeses.

Selective serotonin reuptake inhibitors (SSRIs)

This class of drug, often called the newer generation of antidepressants, blocks the reuptake of serotonin back into the neuron, so that more serotonin can be left in the gap between nerve cells.

Table 1 Antidepressants

Generic drug name	UK trade name	US trade name
Tricyclic antidepressants		
amitriptyline	Tryptizol/Lentizol	Elavil/Endep
clomipramine	Anafranil	Anafranil
desiprimine	Pertofran/Norpramin	Pertofrane/Norpramin
dothiepin (dosulepin)	Prothiaden	--
doxepin	Sinequan	Adapin/Sinequan
imipramine	Tofranil	Tofranil
lofepramine	Gamanil/Lomont	--
nortriptyline	Allegron	Aventil
protriptyline	Concordin	Vivactil
trimipramine	Surmontil	Surmontil
MAOIs (monoamine oxidase inhibitors)		
moclobemide	Mannerix/Aurorix	--
phenelzine	Nardil	Nardil
tranylcypromine	Parnate	Parnate
Serotonin reuptake inhibitors (SSRIs and SNRIs)		
citalopram	Cipramil	Celexa
escitalopram	Lexapro	Lexapro
fluoxetine	Prozac	Prozac
fluvoxamine	Faverin	Luvox
paroxetine	Seroxat	Paxil
sertraline	Lustral	Zoloft
venlafaxine	Efexor	Efexor
Other antidepressants		
buproprion	Zyban – stop smoking	Welbutrin
L-tryptophan	Optimax	Trofan
maprotiline	Ludiomil	Ludiomil
mirtazapine	Zispin	Remeron
nefazodone	Dutonin	Serzone
reboxetine	Edronax	--
trazodone	Molipaxin	Desyrel

Source: Healy, 2002

The idea is that more effective messages can pass between neurons. Side effects of SSRIs include drowsiness, sleep disturbances and nightmares, headaches, jitteriness, tremors and teeth clenching. Less common side effects like akathisia and suicidal ideation can be fatal. Up to one third of people taking SSRIs experience loss of libido and delayed or absent orgasms.

Prozac is the best known SSRI, and was first released in 1988; the word Prozac has since entered our cultural language. Prozac and its relatives are supposed to be safer in overdose than the older antidepressants. Efexor differs from other SSRIs in that it blocks the reuptake of noradrenaline at doses of more than 150 mg. The side effects are similar to other SSRIs and tricyclic antidepressants (TCAs); Efexor can also cause elevated blood pressure. Prolonged use of SSRIs can create dependency, and sudden cessation can cause adverse physical reactions.

Tricyclic antidepressants

TCAs work by blocking reuptake of both serotonin and noradrenaline, and are the 'older generation' of antidepressants. Common side effects are sedation, constipation, urinary retention, dry mouth and blurred vision. More serious side effects are changes in heart rate or rhythm and drop in blood pressure, especially when you stand or sit up suddenly. The first tricyclic was imipramine (Tofranil). Tricyclics can be fatal if you take an overdose.

Serotonin antagonist reuptake inhibitors (SARIs)

This class of drugs (listed under 'Other antidepressants' on page 55) not only reduces the reuptake of serotonin by the neuron that released it but also blocks serotonin receptor sites on the receiving neuron. So more serotonin delivers messages between nerve cells. Side effects include nausea, sedation, jitteriness, blurred vision, constipation and a drop in blood pressure when you suddenly sit or stand up. Dutonin (Serzone in the USA) and Molipaxin (Desyrel in the USA) are trade names for SARIs. Serzone is said to enhance libido, unlike other antidepressants.

Selective norepinephrine reuptake inhibitors (SNRIs)

SNRIs inhibit the reuptake of norepinephrine (also called noradrenaline) in order that more of this neurotransmitter is present at the synapse of neurons. They may also inhibit reuptake of dopamine. Side effects include headache, dry mouth, sleep disturbances, nausea and constipation. Zyban (Welbutrin in the USA) is a well known SNRI, often prescribed to help you stop smoking.

Benzodiazepines

These drugs have been used since the 1970s as sedatives, tranquillizers, muscle relaxants, anticonvulsants and to reduce anxiety. More recently they have been used in the treatment of bipolar disorder. Side effects include drowsiness, dry mouth, constipation, drop in blood pressure when you sit up or stand up, weight gain and sexual dysfunction. They may affect muscle tone and movement (producing Parkinson-like symptoms) and cause restlessness. They are addictive, and made worse with alcohol. 'Benzos' are usually now prescribed only for short periods of time.

Lithium

Lithium is the main drug of choice in treating bipolar disorder. A naturally occurring element, third in the periodic table, lithium is considered unsurpassed in the treatment of bipolarity. It stabilizes mood and helps prevent swings between mania and depression. The statistics seem to bear out that bipolar people on lithium have many fewer suicides than patients not taking the drug. However, many patients cannot tolerate lithium because of 'horrid' side effects. The most common adverse side effects are weight gain, poor memory, tremors, fatigue, thirst, nausea, loss of balance, skin rash and lowered white blood count.

Physical therapies in the treatment of depression

Deep brain stimulation

This therapy is in early stages, and works by planting electrodes in a region near the centre of the brain called Area 25 and sending a steady stream of electric impulses to a pacemaker in the chest. The DBS operation involves an intrusion that is delicate but brutal. Patients are kept awake and given a local anaesthetic so they can describe any changes. The surgical team shaves much of the patient's head and, with four screws drilled through skin into bone, attaches to the skull the stereotactic frame that will hold the head steady against the operating table and serve as a navigational aid. Mounting the frame takes only about 10 minutes, but many patients find this the most distressing part of the whole business, since it involves driving screws into the skull ('You can't truly feel it,' as one patient said, 'but you can hear it and see it and smell it'), and having the steel frame placed around the head. The frame is removed after the operation. There is as yet no real evidence that DBS works.

Electroconvulsive therapy

ECT deserves a longer discussion. It involves sending an electric current through the brain to trigger a seizure, or fit, with the aim, in most cases, of relieving severe depression. The treatment is given under a general anaesthetic (which carries its own risk) and using muscle relaxants, so that the muscles do not contract, and the body does not convulse during the fit. No one seems to be able to give a clear explanation of how ECT works, and this is a cause of controversy. Its critics (and I am one of them) describe it as a crude treatment that can cause brain damage; on the other hand, its supporters defend it as an effective and life-saving technique.

A survey conducted by MIND, in 2001, of mental health service users who had received ECT, reported that as many people found it unhelpful as helpful. One woman said, 'I would happily die rather than have ECT again', while another stated, 'If I had not received ECT I would be dead by now.'

- 36 per cent of those treated in the last five years found it helpful in the short term (within the first six weeks of treatment).
- 27 per cent found it unhelpful or damaging in the short term.
- 43 per cent felt that it was unhelpful or damaging in the long term.

Two-thirds of all those asked, and almost half of those who had

had ECT in the last two years, would not agree to have it again. The author Ernest Hemingway committed suicide shortly after ECT treatment at the Mayo Clinic in 1961. He is reported to have said, 'Well, what is the sense of ruining my head and erasing my memory, which is my capital, and putting me out of business? It was a brilliant cure but we lost the patient.'

Studies in 2004 and 2005 showed that half of ECT patients did not feel that they could refuse the treatment. In the UK, ECT is largely administered to the elderly and disadvantaged, and patients are predominantly female. Psychiatrists who never find it necessary to use ECT are numerous, as are those who administer it with the greatest caution. Whichever side of the debate one takes up, it is fair to say that ECT represents the 'faulty-machine-physical-disease' approach to mental illness. A large number of interested parties consider the use of ECT to be ineffective and barbaric. Advocates of ECT, however, present the alternative view that depression can be debilitating, and that taking risks is part of saving lives; to ban the use of ECT would be, they say, to condemn some severely depressed individuals to continued despair.

In the UK, ECT can only be given without consent if you are detained in hospital under the Mental Health Act 1983, and this is authorized by a doctor appointed by the Mental Health Act Commission (a second opinion appointed doctor, or SOAD). This doctor must visit you and consult with your own doctor, a nurse, and another professional involved in your care who is neither a doctor nor a nurse. The only exception to this is in an emergency. In such cases, treatment can begin, under section 62 of the Act, pending the arrival of the SOAD, for patients without capacity to consent, in a life-threatening situation, where the common law might be invoked. The risks of ECT, according to the US Food and Drug Administration, include brain damage and memory loss.

Light therapy

Light therapy is used to treat SAD, or seasonal affective disorder, and is self-descriptive. Seasons of the year affect mood, and we can become low when we lack sunshine and the days grow shorter. The depression attending SAD can be debilitating and even life-threatening. Banks of light can help lift depression. The method is low-cost, simple, low-tech, and as far as I have been able to ascertain, safe to use.

Repetitive transcranial magnetic stimulation (RTMS)

This involves the application of magnets to the right side of the brain, producing a localized weak magnetic field in the interest of alleviating depression. The procedure does not require sedation and the patient is not made uncomfortable, and there appears to be no loss of memory. Convulsions do occur with the application of a stronger magnetic field, and convulsive TMS is in an experimental stage at the time of writing.

Vagus nerve stimulation

The vagus nerve is a cranial nerve. It is the principal component of the parasympathetic division of the autonomic nervous system. It passes from the *medulla oblongata* (in the brainstem) through the neck and chest to the abdomen. It has branches to a number of major organs including the larynx, pharynx, trachea, lungs, heart and digestive system. Stimulation of the vagus nerve increases the level of neurotransmitters like serotonin. This treatment is experimental, but is said to alleviate depression in some. A small electrical device is implanted under the skin on the left chest, a bit like a cardiac pacemaker, and connected to the left vagus nerve in the neck. The device sends a small current to the vagus nerve for 30 seconds every 5 minutes, 24 hours a day.

The physical model of diagnosing mental disorders

Medicine has come to favour natural science as the fundamental cause of mental irregularities, and the standard tool used for such diagnoses is *DSM-IV*, or *The Diagnostic and Statistical Manual of Mental Disorders*. The original *Diagnostic and Statistical Manual of Mental Disorders* (1952) contained 107 mental health disorders. By the fourth edition (1994), entries had more than trebled, to 365. The DSM is the bible of the psychiatric trade. It is constantly being updated; there were three new editions in one 14-year period, and the next edition is in preparation during the writing of this book. Each new edition means that every therapist, library, insurance company and government employee has to buy the new one, which brings millions of dollars in profits to the publisher, the American Psychiatric Association. Some of the entries in the manual give considerable cause for concern, particularly in moderate circles. *DSM-V*, projected for publication in 2010, will undoubtedly contain many more new disorders.

One example is 'premenstrual dysphoric disorder' or PMDD (*DSM-IV*, 1994). Some sources claim that premenstrual mental disorder (which entered *DSM* in 1985) was invented by two men on a fishing trip. We're not talking here about bloating and breast tenderness and some irritability – what once was meant by 'premenstrual syndrome' – but rather a *mental disorder*. No sooner had *DSM* listed this new mental disability than the Food and Drug Administration approved the use of Prozac to treat this new disease. Enter Sarafem, daughter of Prozac. In the first seven months following approval, Sarafem was prescribed to more than 200,000 patients in the USA. Meanwhile the European Union's drug regulator, the Committee for Proprietary Medicinal Products, found that PMDD was not a well-established entity. Health professionals in Europe were instructed to stop prescribing Prozac/Sarafem for that 'condition'. No such steps were taken in the USA. Thus arose a curious phenomenon: Sarafem will work with American women but not European women.

Another new condition is 'intermittent explosive disorder', for which read 'anger'. Then there is 'inhibited male orgasm'. Remember these are classed as mental disorders.

Thoughts on medication

What are the pros and cons of treating depression as a disease? Of taking psychiatric drugs? What are the pros and cons of reducing or coming off medication? How do psychiatric drugs affect people?

People deserve more information about psychiatric drugs and more opportunities to think and talk about wide-ranging issues relating to medication. If you've read this far in a chapter that is somewhat less than light entertainment, you are most likely one of these people, and the following chapters will provide more helpful information on the subject. Despite assurances from the pharmaceutical industry that many drugs are non-addictive and do not have withdrawal problems or serious adverse reactions, very many people have experienced sometimes extreme difficulties, both while taking them, and when trying to come off antidepressant medication. If you are depressed, and most of us will be to some degree at some stage in our lives, you deserve reliable information and support.

- Accurate information about these drugs.
- The provision of support in a safe and friendly environment where there is respect for your opinion.
- Access to expertise from various sources, e.g. people who offer complementary therapies.
- Help from people who can give you an honest assessment of pros and cons of medications.
- Help from people to think about alternative ways of recovering.
- Advice and support for people who decide to reduce or come off drugs, including accurate advice regarding withdrawal reactions.

5

Bringing the dog to 'heal':
case studies

The term 'clinical depression' finds its way into too many conversations these days. One has a sense that a catastrophe has occurred in the psychic landscape.

(Leonard Cohen)

Madness is a label that other people put on to someone who is suffering immense mental distress, someone who just isn't able to cope. If we understood how we operate as humans then we would understand that madness doesn't exist; it's just a way of feeling when we discover that there's a serious discrepancy between what we thought our life was and what actually is.

(Dorothy Rowe, 'This much I know',
Observer, 1 September 2002)

My long-time friend and I are having a leisurely lunch of jacket potatoes with baked beans and cheese; we've just been horse riding at a local riding school. I mention this book. 'When depression hit me for the second time,' she said, 'it was visible and physical. I was 35 years old, I'd been working too hard, travelling too far to work, and having literally disabling pain with my monthly periods. The doctor pooh-poohed the menstrual problem, but it was the kind of crippling pain that caused vomiting and sent me to bed for five days every month. Self-worth has never been my strongest point and I came to losing my sense of clarity and confidence.

'One morning at home, and at the lowest ebb, I remember planning my demise, simultaneously feeling horrified at myself for harbouring this impulse. I needed to flee from it, *now*. I was in my nightdress, barefoot. I walked into the field below our house, literally running away from the part of me who wanted to die. As I walked across the field, I saw in the distance and coming towards me an amorphous blob, like a swarm of bees in that it moved towards me and sideways too, even as I tried to dodge it. I was transfixed. It kept coming and eventually was "in my face". It entered my forehead and settled in my skull, its tentacles clasping my brain. I felt a tightening in my scalp and a dull relentless pressure.

'My husband helped me write some notes on what had happened to me to take to our doctor. I recall that the surgery nurse was kind; but when the doctor "saw" me, she avoided my eyes. She read my notes, asked the nurse to fetch the MIMMS [the doctor's prescribing guidelines], and then addressed me via the nurse and in the third person. She prescribed a hormone of some sort. I realized at that point that I was truly on my own and would have to heal myself. It took three years but I did gradually recover with lots of help from family and friends.'

Plus, I can testify, huge dollops of remarkable courage and determination! My friend's earlier experience of depression happened when she was in her twenties; she simply found it impossible to work. Then she couldn't stop crying. Her flatmate at the time booked an appointment for her, and this doctor proved sympathetic, practical and expert. When she said, 'There's nothing wrong with me', even as she was in floods of tears, the kindly doctor said, 'But look at you!' He prescribed a tricyclic antidepressant and booked her in for weekly talk sessions with him to mark her progress. So it was her best friend, and her doctor at that time, who gave life-reviving help with weekly counselling appointments supplemented with medication. The medications gave her a breathing space, and much-needed sleep; and the doctor's insistence on weekly catch-ups meant that my friend recovered her strength, her state of well-being, and a promising career. Importantly, she was not on a drug regime long enough for the dangers of addiction to kick in. I couldn't help wondering whether the sort of GP who helped her then could possibly exist in the present climate of the UK NHS.

Drugs can help us through life; these include not only medications, but coffee, tea, alcohol and herbal remedies. I have respected friends who have decided to abstain from some or all of these, but I am not one of them. Like the earlier generation of amphetamines usually prescribed for obesity problems, the newer generation of antidepressant medications can create a lift in mood and enhance a person's sense of well-being, as do other 'uppers' such as amphetamines, cocaine, Ecstasy, all of which act on the same serotonin pathway. Many people claim that it was the drug rather than their own resources that got them through a bad depressive 'patch'. One of my friends said, 'I felt a surge of energy. I felt clear and "clean", and I was confident and relaxed at work. I began to enjoy life again.' Another experienced a physical 'lifting' of pain from her forehead after being prescribed an antidepressant as she tried to recover from a painful divorce. Yet another is convinced that Prozac quite simply saved his life. It is, however, worth remembering the placebo effect. It has been clearly demonstrated that the placebo effect – which is a demonstration of trust (see Chapter 6) – equals or outperforms the effect of drugs across the board, and with no disturbing side effects.

All of us respond to human interaction – when we are depressed and emotionally distressed, our response is often ultra-sensitive and extreme. Some of the people whose stories appear in this chapter are friends; others have contacted me via Prozac and antidepressants alert networks, or are those I have encountered through national and international networks. Some have asked that their names be changed. All the stories are true and unembellished. Chosen from hundreds of cases, these stories represent the resilience and courage of the human spirit to heal and rebuild. The bias leans towards an anti-drug perspective for two reasons: (a) because of adverse reactions, drugs have become problematic as a first line of treatment for depression, and (b) the people who don't respond well to drug treatment are the people who have sought my advice and help.

Caveat. Taking or not taking medication is a personal matter. If you are being treated with any of the medications mentioned in the following narratives, do not cease taking them without first discussing your concerns with your doctor or with someone who is qualified to discuss adverse drug reactions and willing to listen to your concerns. It can be dangerous to stop taking antidepressant medications suddenly. (See Appendix 1.)

Luke

Luke and his wife Lynn, in their early thirties, had been happily married for nine years. Luke had no history of any kind of mental or depressive illness. However, after a bereavement in the family and other simultaneous and distressing events, he felt he was having some sort of crisis and went to see his GP in hopes of being prescribed something to help. The GP told Luke that he could see that he was a 'very anxious man' and suggested that he took paroxetine (Seroxat in the UK, Paxil in the USA), starting off on 20 mg/day. He also prescribed beta-blockers 50 mg/day, to steady Luke's palpitations.

The following morning Luke took one 20 mg Seroxat tablet (along with a beta-blocker). Throughout the day he felt steadily worse. He felt he had no control over his thoughts or actions and the panicky/jittery feelings were growing far more intense (the term for this drug-induced state is akathisia). The tension became too great for Luke, and later in the day he attempted suicide by cutting his neck and wrists. Thankfully Lynn found Luke in time, although Luke ended up in intensive care and in a critical condition.

Lynn stressed that Luke had *never* attempted suicide before, or since. He stated firmly to all the doctors, nurses and psychiatrists that he didn't have any suicidal thoughts before taking Seroxat and didn't harbour any such feelings afterwards. He did say, though, that after taking the 20 mg tablet he lost all control over his thoughts and actions, and was extremely frightened by the thoughts that assaulted him. He had never taken any illegal drugs but imagined that the way he felt when he cut himself was probably like being on a terrible 'trip'.

Luke and Lynn reported Luke's reaction, under the Yellow Card System, to the British Committee on the Safety of Medicines. According to the ADROIT database there had been at least 32 cases of obsessive suicidal thinking reported in association with paroxetine (this was in 2001); obviously only those who made the connection between the drug and the extreme effects reported via the Yellow Card System. Luke's reaction to the drug is very rare in that it occurred so soon after the first tablet, but it is now reliably estimated that between 2 and 10 per cent of patients experience a spectrum of disturbing/dangerous adverse effects to SSRI and SNRI medications.

Luke's recovery is inspiring. A gifted artist, through his own courage and the devotion of his partner he has set up a company. I was able to obtain from him an early commission which now graces our home. Recently Lynn and Luke have had a baby.

Helen

At the age of nine Helen was diagnosed with chronic psychotic disorder. This diagnosis served as an umbrella for everything from psychotic bipolar depression through emerging 'cluster B personality pathology'. Helen's most painful memories from this time are of feelings of parental abandonment and of a 'pin-down' by three male psychiatric nurses in an isolation ward.

Helen generously observed that those treating her did not know what harm they were doing. They couldn't understand the invalidation, the horrible effects of the drugs on her ability to think rationally, or that she was traumatized by the physical coercion involved in her treatment.

Her cries of pain were ignored. Instead, Helen was told she lacked insight and needed to take responsibility for her actions. Helen agreed that she needed to be responsible, but her carers' denial of the harm and the pain she felt led to an impasse.

Helen firmly believes that most of the issues she faced in her eight years as a patient, between the ages of 8 and 16, were made worse by the system itself.

Helen's message to mental health providers is simple and important: to understand that they can cause harm. She thinks that as healers, they do not want to believe they do cause harm. Helen left the system at 18. With solid support from family, counsellors and friends, she has now lived free of all psychoactive medications for four years and has a healthy outlook on life. Helen campaigns actively against involuntary treatment. She builds websites. When depression hits, as she now believes it hits most of us, she knows how to deal with it.

Jerome

I sat at the top of the stairs, frowned upon by the recently painted deep pink woodchip stretching down three flights of stairs to the front door. I contemplated the intended fall, trying to decide whether it was far enough or sure enough to end my miserable existence. The softness of the carpet, the risk of damaging the hundred freshly painted jade spindles – finished at about 4 a.m. – and the difficulty of successfully negotiating the bends, persuaded me that this was not a valid mode of suicide. The considering of an alternative, more efficient method was enough to break the spell; I realized I had a problem.

This was one of the low points, but only one of many that now seem as if they happened to someone else, someone who was incomplete and incapable of living life as an adult. Many years, hundreds of antidepressant pills and hours of counselling later, I can begin to unravel what led me to that place and how I emerged, stronger, far more alive and ready to face each day with an inner belief in my ability to cope and make a positive contribution to the world.

A few days after contemplating suicide, I took myself to the local GP. I was surprised that she was willing to consider my breakdown from all possible angles and not just put it down to the pressures of teaching in a difficult school in inner London. In fact she was happy to admit that she had no idea of the cause and made a triple prescription: time off work, counselling and Prozac.

I took my daily dose of Prozac for the next three years. At the time she explained all about serotonin, how brains react during depression and the change Prozac would bring. To this day I still wonder if it did anything at all. I faithfully took my medicine – which was easy – and tried to deal with the root causes of my illness through counselling – which was incredibly hard and painful. Looking back, Prozac was just something I took on prescription in blind faith that it would help and continued to take daily until I felt I was strong enough to live without it. I felt no different the day I popped the first pill, apart from misplaced pride in being on the latest 'trendy' drug, right up to the days after I stopped taking them. Perhaps Prozac helped create a small window of opportunity which allowed me to see a possible path ahead, a future worth being part of, a world which was not necessarily better without me. Then again, perhaps it did nothing at all.

I write this account, 12 years later, and look back at the small frightened child who took over my life. He is still with me today and at times still tries to take over, overwhelming my emotions with simple reactions based on terror and worthlessness. Now I can recognize and acknowledge these feelings, and fight my way out of the churning whirlpool which threatens to engulf me. I have been there and confronted my darkest fears and know I am not alone. I am not defined by that child alone, but also by the capable, mature adult which is another part of my reality, a part that is strong enough, big enough and valuable enough to continue, and caring enough to look after that child.

Did Prozac help me to get to this place? The truth is I am not sure. My mentor and friend along this journey was my counsellor, Ann, a woman I alternately wanted to be my mother, my childhood friend and my lover, a woman who stood and sat beside me as I discovered a sense of adult self-worth while acknowledging the frightened little boy who will be a part of me for ever.

That small child was in charge of my emotions for many years. It was he who met and fell in love with the mother of my first three daughters, and it was he who insisted on allowing her every freedom within our relationship, freedom which ultimately she could not deal with and which she fled to bind herself within a controlling and safe partnership, taking my wonderful children with her. She now has no idea of how I've grown and is perplexed by reactions that are no longer those she expects. I have no way to reach her past the hurt and bitterness, and no desire to do so. My more complete self would never have fallen for her then, and now struggles to untangle the love I feel for our children from the intense disappointment and disgust the child within, and I as a whole, continue to feel at her actions.

Unlike my use of Prozac, my counselling continued for many years until after the break-up of my marriage, just over eight years ago. After a brief and admittedly 'rebound relationship', I was able to move on and, for the first time, not take on every hurt as my fault.

I am now in an adult relationship, the first of my life. I have two more wonderful daughters and an amazingly grown-up and passionate wife. The child who sat at the top of the stairs is still with me, and at times still needs to be cared for and looked after, but now I am able to incorporate that part of me into a greater whole. The part Prozac played in my journey is still unclear. Would I be here now without it? The truth is I do not know. But here I am, and here I intend to stay. Now I know I deserve to live and have something to give, and the future will happen with me a definite part of it because I matter. And the world is, just possibly, a better place with me in it, than without me.

Susan

I never even thought of, let alone described, myself as 'depressed' until my mother died in May 2004. She was 89 and had what was by any standards a 'peaceful end' to a mercifully short period of failing health.

For me, her 61-year-old daughter, to note in her diary three months later that I found myself 'seriously, perhaps clinically depressed', might suggest two things, the first being that I have lived a very sheltered life. I have been blessed with good health and much happiness but I have also had and seen many troubles in my life, the worst being the death (in 1999) of my much loved husband, father of our four children, after 35 years of marriage.

Although I am untrained in the mental health field myself, I am surrounded by experts, my eldest son for one. He works for a mental health charity called Rethink. My husband's brother was in and out of various mental hospitals all his life, as were many others we knew through my husband's work as an Anglican priest. He had, for 14 years of his working life, served in a parish in London well known for being the epicentre of mental health guru-dom.

So, assuming I know what the term depression means, why did I apply it to myself on this one occasion? How could my mother's 'happy release' induce this condition when a far more traumatic passing had not? It was, I've realized, because there was nothing essentially 'wrong' with my husband's death, despite its suddenness and untimeliness. It was inexpressibly sad, of course, not just for me and our children, but for all our friends; crucially, we all saw it through together.

My mother's death, on the other hand, brought out the worst in my father and siblings. The parental favouritism that had scarred our family life over the years now threatened to tear it apart completely.

The catalyst for this breakdown was my older brother, my mother's firstborn, being excluded from her deathbed at the instigation of a favoured younger sister whom he had displeased. My brother's exclusion was set in stone with the will my mother had signed (under duress? She was quite poorly and her signature very wobbly) excluding that same son not just from a share in her estate but from the record of her life.

The treatment I received from those who had placed themselves in charge of my mother's memorializing was mild in comparison to my brother's, but it had the same effect, which was to exclude and prevent me from mourning my mother as I needed to do and as she deserved.

I was helped in locating this as the source of my depression by a friend, a sturdy witty woman with a loving husband and two wonderful children, who had been through the same thing when her father died (at 92 and suffering from Alzheimer's). She became so deeply depressed as to require medical help over many months. I was glad to have been on hand for support during this time, little knowing that comparing notes when I was in the same boat five years later was to be a crucial part of my own healing.

Alongside this gift of wisdom arrived Shakespeare. Was it grace or luck that led the video of Kenneth Branagh's film production of *Hamlet* to be returned to me after five years' 'borrowing'? I fell upon the video as a means of taking my mind off seemingly insoluble problems, but found in it the key to understanding and hope-fully – I'm not there yet – resolving them.

Oceans of ink have been written about the noble Prince's plight: was he mad? Or just pretending to be? Was he simply, as popular theorists of the 1960s proclaimed, a disaffected youth? 'A pox on all these interpretations!' Branagh's film proclaims. Hamlet had fallen into a state that people of his time would have termed a melan-choly, one so deep that he can no longer see any beauty or meaning in the world – soul-sick if you like (which I do); if this isn't what depression is, I've understood nothing about my own condition or anybody else's.

Hamlet knows that fathers die, just as my good friend and I did. We would have agreed with Hamlet's mother's reminder that such things are 'common'. So 'why seems it so particular, with thee?' she asks. Because of treachery, the Prince doesn't reply, but he knows. He is troubled because his father's death was 'out of joint' and had put the whole world out of joint.

Just as I was troubled at my mother's death. I am no nobly born hero charged with vengeance of a murdered parent. But if – and some of the wisest experts on the subject suggest this to be the case – a key source of depression can be the loss of a relationship, then Hamlet and I are both witnesses to/survivors of a loss that had become 'particular', indeed tragic, through being dis-ordered.

It's not the falling out within the family that troubled me: those relationships can, in theory, be mended. Where there's life, there is, or ought to be, hope. There is hope in death too, for while death ends a life it doesn't end a relationship. But it is a different kind of hope, one in which the relationship continues solely because of and through remembering the love that was there on earth. However, some deaths make continuing and sustaining the loving relationship harder. I want to know Mum is OK. I know my husband is, but I'm not sure she is. That is, in every sense of the word, depressing. My depression has lifted but the familial alien-ation is a continuing and all too common story.

Cordelia

Cordelia spends much of her life in the public eye. Her experience of misdiagnosis as depressive occurred in America, where multiple-choice questionnaires appear to have become common tools of diagnosing mental health problems, and where Columbia University has devised a mental health screening test commonly known as Teen Screen [see Appendix 2]. The test Cordelia describes below would not be dissimilar to Teen Screen.

In the autumn of 2003, I had a mental evaluation at the Mayo Clinic, because although I was physically ill, no one could find an accurate diagnosis. The doctor wanted to be sure that my condition wasn't from psychological sources. The psychiatrist, her trainee and I had an hour's consultation, resulting in the declaration of a clean bill of health and suggesting that at most I might consider a women's support group on returning home. This is standard practice at the Mayo. Then they asked me to fill out a two-page multiple-choice test.

The next day, my senior doctor called me in for an emergency appointment, explaining that the psychiatrist's office had put me on the alert for 'depression and at high risk of suicide'. This was alarming news, not least because my main doctor (an infectious disease specialist and immunologist) responded with a cocktail of copious drugs, and immediately set me up for another visit with a psychiatrist (at $500/£300) an hour.

I smelled a rat. I said, as calmly as I could, 'I believe I know why the evaluators have come to such a conclusion. Do you not find it strange that your multiple-choice test should contradict your own opinion, your own eyes, your own sense of my well-being, after we talked for an hour?'

'Yes,' she said, 'I did wonder about that.'

'May I tell you what I think has happened?'

'That would be helpful. Sure.'

'The first tricky question asked if I felt people were talking about me. I wrote yes, because: (1) I see six or seven different doctors a day. They are naturally talking about me and how I am going to get better. (2) I know that family and friends are worried and talking about me. At least I hope so. (3) I just heard that the *San Francisco Chronicle* had done a story on the most under-recognized talents of the twentieth century. I was in it. I'm an actress. People talk about me. (4) I've written an article, and my agent called to tell me that it's going to be published. She and the publishers talk about me.'

She stopped me. 'Okay, I get it. And the other questions?'

'The second question that bothered me asked if I think people are laughing at me. The honest answer is yes. I do silly things on purpose all the time. It's the performing artist in me. Not long before I sat the test, I was singing at the piano in the main lobby; a little boy came by to sing with me. People began to gather round, laughing and having a great time. So yes, I do think people laugh at me and I like it that way!'

'Good point.' My psychiatrist started laughing, herself.

'And now the big monster question,' I said. 'The test asked if I had thought of suicide in the last seven days. Do you recall that there was a great deal of coverage about Terri Schiavo and the right to die? [*Terri Schiavo was in a coma for several years after respiratory and cardiac arrest. Her husband eventually asked that artificial life support be withdrawn, against her family's wishes, and the case became a subject of international media coverage and debates about euthanasia and suicide.*] An elderly man was showing me the article, and we got into a long discussion around what we would do if confronted with a loved one in a permanent vegetative state. Then we moved on to different cultures and suicide. So, yes, I had recently thought of suicide. Not of committing it NOW, or maybe even ever, but I *thought* of suicide in the last several days.'

The doctor was amazed. She then asked, 'How did you know that it was those three questions that led to the evaluation?'

I answered, 'Doctor, it was obvious when I was answering them. I chose to answer truthfully, when in fact all this could have been avoided, had I lied, which at the time, I did think was the smarter thing to do. One problem: I don't lie! Whatever gave anyone the thought that a human being could be evaluated as mentally ill or mentally stable, healthy or not, from two pages of multiple-choice questions? Who is responsible for that kind of hubris?'

The doctor apologized. 'I have to say I agree with you. We avoid multiple choice even in college tests nowadays. They are highly inaccurate in ascertaining the testers' knowledge of the test-taker's reasoning while making complex choices.' She then assured me that she would call my doctor and remove the diagnosis from my record.

I am telling this true story to show how misleading, even how *dangerous* these tests can be. Many people will not be equipped to fight as hard as I did. These tests were stopped for many years, and must be stopped once again, this time for good.

(Author's note: During my last stay in a hospital for a surgical procedure, I diligently filled in a multiple-choice test asking questions about my emotional state. I did not discover the way in which this information has been used.)

Rosie

'I was 17 years old, and in the middle of studying for my college exams. I was also studying classical piano at the Royal College of

Music in London. I was extremely happy and I had my whole life ahead of me.

I went to the doctor because I was feeling tired and anxious. When he recommended an antidepressant, I laughed and told him I was not depressed – but he told me it would make me feel 'that little bit better'. I did not take it at first but a few months later I was still feeling somewhat tired. I went back to my doctor who again advised me to take antidepressants. He said to me, 'If you will not take my advice then do not come and see me.' I took his advice.

But I developed disturbing symptoms. I began to burn all over, as if my whole body were on fire. I still suffer from this pain from time to time, and it is agonizing. I cannot go anywhere because I can only cope with the pain if I am in a cold room (normal places and normal temperatures are unbearable). I can no longer enjoy the sun because of this burning. It literally feels as if there is acid all over me, burning my skin.

Another immediate physical symptom was for my entire body to swell with fluid. I also still suffer from this at present. I look like a different person when I am like this. My face is at times so

swollen I cannot see properly as there is so much fluid around my eyes. My whole body is like this. I took Cipramil for six weeks. I was extremely unwell by this time. I suffered stabbing pains in my head and body (as if someone were stabbing me with a sharp knife), shooting pains in my eyes, head and body, severe sickness, mood swings, confusion, difficulty breathing and severe chest pains. Following the advice of my doctor, I stopped taking the medication – not gradually, but abruptly. I was told it was not the medication causing these problems, but if I wanted to stop it then stop it. Later on, the doctor prescribed different antidepressants at increased dosages, to treat the symptoms I had developed while on my original medication.

Sadly things got worse. The physical symptoms continued to persist. I began to get extremely high temperatures, followed later by temperatures as low as 90 degrees. My resting pulse was and still is constantly racing at 120–150 beats per minute and I suffered breathlessness. I also began to get very strange feelings, as if my head had fallen off. I would tell myself it couldn't have fallen off, yet it physically felt as though it really had. I would have to feel my head with my hands to know it was still connected to my neck – ridiculous, but true, and there was a constant electrical buzzing inside my head.

Throughout this time I continued to take the medication. When the burning got worse, the doctor put me on Prozac. The fluid around my body increased. Mood swings became uncontrollable and unbearable. I wasn't on Prozac very long before I tried to come off it gradually. I have now been off Prozac since September 2004.

While on Prozac I had terrible nightmares. Very often I didn't know whether I had just had another of the dreams, or whether it had actually happened. One time I found an empty paracetamol box in my room. I had no idea why it was there or whether or not I had actually taken the pills. It was the most frightening thing not knowing or being able to remember what had happened. My parents took me to hospital for treatment, and it was found that I had taken the pills.

Since ceasing antidepressants, I fear I have lost confidence in my prescribing physician who appeared to blame and even disbelieve me for the side effects I experienced. I have continued with adverse symptoms and suffered from hyperaemia (low potassium). This condition became very severe for some time. But this year (2006) I had a glimpse of what it feels like to be well again. I'm not saying everything's a bowl of cherries, but I continue to feel better and am getting my life back again. I am realistic; all I now wish for is to get better and to at least have some kind of normal life again.

Rosie has recently discovered an interest in the field of NLP (neuro-linguistic programming) and is working as a waitress in order to help fund her studies. She has just received an NLP diploma certification and intends to become a qualified NLP practitioner. Rosie now sees her future as positive and full of possibilities. She hopes to work specifically with people withdrawing from psychiatric medications. Her aim is eventually to open her own clinic, which she hopes will be unique in therapy and completely drug-free.

Cecilia

Cecilia's depression and anxiety began when final exams at university approached. She confesses to being a perfectionist, as are other family members; and to a fear of failure. At the time she withdrew into a shell and had overwhelming feelings of power-lessness. She went to her GP who prescribed Prozac, which her doctor described as the 'magic bullet of your generation'. At first she felt terrible, suffering the jitters, teeth clenching, nightmares, insomnia and palpitations. But as the doctor had predicted, these symptoms subsided and Cecilia began to experience a calmness. She managed her exam preps and started going out with friends. At the same time she felt what she described as 'a sort of flatline emotional distance' from everything. Taking Prozac became a routine part of everyday life. When the times arose and she felt like stopping the drug, a crisis would pop up and Cecilia would keep taking the tablets.

As time passed, however, Cecilia found Prozac no longer staved off feeling low, especially when something unhappy-making occurred with her boyfriend or job. When she mentioned this to her doctor, the doctor reflected that Cecilia would probably need to take Prozac for the rest of her life, a thought which she found distressing.

Cecilia was determined not to be dependent on antidepressant medication for life and, most interestingly, thinks it may have been her decision to take up paragliding which has made all the difference to her recovery. After her first expedition, she decided to wean herself off, using reliable withdrawal protocols (see Appendix 1). She realized that the drug was no more than a block on her deepest feelings. Cecilia gradually came off the drug, and went to see a holistic counsellor, who helped trace the roots of her fears and unhappiness. She knows that life will throw some wild cards and even possibly tragedy, and continues to build inner resources to cope.

Jay

Jay Neugeboren is the acclaimed author of several works of fiction and non-fiction. His brother Robert experienced his first mental distress (diagnosed as manic depression and schizophrenia) during his freshman year at university and has continued to suffer the horrors of mental illness for 40 years. Jay has been Robert's primary carer through these years. In 2002 a film was made telling Jay and Robert's story: Imagining Robert: My Brother, Madness and Survival *<www.imaginingrobert.org>.*

By 1998, Jay Neugeboren's brother Robert had been a patient in the mental-health system for nearly 40 years, and had been given nearly every antipsychotic medication known to humankind.

When Robert's doctor put him on an atypical antipsychotic, Robert's reaction to the drug was very positive. Several months after he started taking it, his psychiatrist rang to say his recovery was nothing short of miraculous – he was clear thinking, free of delusions, and the hospital was planning his discharge. Sadly the euphoria was short-lived.

A few weeks later, Robert telephoned his brother. 'Alan's leaving – Alan's leaving!' he kept screaming. Alan was Robert's social worker, and they had been friends for many years. Without warning Alan had been transferred to another hospital. Soon after Alan's departure Robert began having tantrums, hallucinations, bodily tremors, irrational fears, panic attacks, and also became both dangerously manic *and* depressed. The anguished question which Jay posed was this: why did the medication that worked so well suddenly stop working? His answer: Robert was deprived of a relationship that had been a crucial element in his recovery.

During this time, Jay had been researching for a book. He interviewed literally hundreds of people who had been diagnosed and hospitalized for mental health problems often for 10 years or more, and had recovered to lead full lives. Jay asked them all what had made the difference to their recovery. Some said they found God; some said medications, new and old; some mentioned a particular programme; but no matter what else they believed made a difference, every single person said that a key element of recovery was a relationship with a human being.

Most frequently, this human being was a professional carer – a social worker, a nurse, a doctor, or member of the clergy; sometimes it was a family member. In every single case, it was the presence of an individual who said, 'I believe you will be able to recover, and I intend to be there for you', that brought them back.

This was the case with Robert, who through his daily collaboration with Alan and the dedication of his psychiatrist (who refused to go along with the consensus that Robert would never live independently) has not had a recurrence for more than six years, the longest stretch in his adult life.

The professional carers who stewarded Robert's return to normality believe that pills, while useful, are only a small part of the story, and that the more we emphasize medications as key to recovery, the more we overlook what is at least as important: people working with people on a sustained long-term basis.

Jay Neugeboren is not an extremist. He advocates continued research into effective medications, but linked inextricably with the most essential resource of all: fellow human beings upon whom to depend to guide through the dark times and, once through, to emerge, in Jay's words, into 'gloriously imperfect lives'.

Winifred

Winifred knew the cause of her feelings of depression. Her boyfriend had just told her he didn't love her any more. Not long after this difficult news, and as she was beginning a new relationship, she discovered she was pregnant. She was 21 and she wanted to keep the baby. Terrible morning sickness meant missing work, and Winifred got sacked from her job. Within a few days she found herself with an emergency referral for psychiatric help. By this time she was four months pregnant.

The psychiatrist prescribed an antidepressant. By chance and on the evening following this appointment, Winifred saw a television programme which seemed to affirm her instincts that antidepressants would not be helpful to this wanted new life. She went back to her GP explaining her concerns. The doctor said not to worry and advised Winifred to take the medication as prescribed by the psychiatrist.

Winifred took her worries to her trusted grandmother, who listened and then advised her to follow her instincts. Winifred felt that she trusted her instincts but needed also to take a good hard look at herself and confront her demons too. With her grandmother's acceptance, love and support, Winifred changed her diet, took up yoga, and practised her own version of positive thinking. She began to cope better gradually, and is grateful for her healthy intuition and wise grandmother. She has a healthy baby girl.

Ben

Ben was going through a confusing time in his life. He had been getting over a bad relationship and was losing weight too rapidly. His doctor prescribed the antidepressant Faverin (Luvox in the USA).

At first Ben suffered tremors and nightmares, but he persisted with the medication and within a few weeks noticed that he felt happier, always cheerful. He liked this feeling of sleeping better, feeling rested and just 'good' about life in general, even though he confessed to feeling 'just a bit superficial'.

By the end of the third month on the drug, however, Ben began to think the tablets had done their work and that he didn't need them any more. Very ill-advisedly, he stopped taking them abruptly. He described this point as the beginning of a seemingly interminable descending spiral that, in his words, he 'would not wish on anybody'. He began having 'unwanted and abnormal thoughts'. When he contacted PANTS.UK, he was having constant thoughts of violence and self-harm. He was afraid to leave his house, although he did manage to hold down his job. He hated the company even of his closest friends. He became frightened of his PlayStation and felt he was a 'stranger in my own body', and could not control who he was.

Ben was shocked that his doctor didn't know that his adverse reactions were well-documented withdrawal effects of the drug he had taken. It took more than six months to emerge from these side effects, and more than a year to return to his old, normal self. But Ben did it, with support from friends and with psychotherapy. He is training to be a teacher of English as a second language.

Frederick

Frederick found that he couldn't stop weeping after the death of Elsie, his wife of 70 years. The doctor prescribed antidepressants and Frederick stopped crying. Over the following months, however, Frederick seemed to slow down; in his daughter's words, to 'zombie-fy'; he stopped caring about eating or seeing family and friends. Previously a dapper dresser with strict habits of hygiene, Frederick stopped caring about his appearance too.

He was a man with a sharp and intuitive mind; his family put down these behavioural changes to a natural consequence of old age and of mourning. But his daughter Valerie was concerned, and asked if he thought the medications might be affecting his behaviour. Frederick ignored the question by drifting off into silence.

It was Frederick's granddaughter who asked him what medication he was taking. It turned out that it was the same prescription drug that she had been given for postnatal depression and she observed to Frederick that after a time she felt like 'a zombie', and weaned herself off with the help of her doctor. She persuaded Frederick to think about doing likewise, and went to the doctor with her grandfather for advice. The doctor was caring and sympathetic and observed that Frederick's symptoms could be among the adverse reactions to his medication. She worked out a regime for taking Frederick off the medication. In a matter of weeks, Frederick was back to previous energy levels. He still wept and mourned and missed his beloved Elsie, but why not? He said to me that he could

not believe that he sat in his chair for all those months just staring
into space.

Rod

Rod had always believed and practised in his life that nothing could
beat depression like exercise, diet, meditation, good healthy sex,
and holidays. He had also over the years handled bouts of severe
depression with counselling and a healthy lifestyle. But when his
partner of 20 years left him for someone else, Rod's life crashed
around him and he asked his doctor for an antidepressant.

The initial release from stress and anxiety and literally gut-
wrenching pain was spectacular and positive. Rod chose to stay on
the medication and only after two years decided to try the drug-free
route by cutting down gradually on his medication. He found that
when he tried to stop taking it altogether, to go down from 5 mg to
zero, he could not do so. The major reaction was what he described
as 'zapping' in his head, or 'swooshes' in his brain.

Rod decided to go back on the medication at a stabilizing level
in order to restore what he calls 'quality life'. The positive effects
are still with him at the time of writing, although he has come full
circle, back to believing that no drug beats a healthy relationship,
laughter, diet and exercise.

John

I was diagnosed with depression leading up to leaving a long-
serving job in the media. I refused the GP's offer of drugs, feeling
that my depression was situational – not just about the horrors
of working in the department I was in, but also midlife transition
and the rigours of working in another job based at home. I could
see that feeling 'artificially' better might help me to cope and
work through these difficulties, but I wasn't sure about it; just like
getting drunk doesn't solve your financial worries, so feeling better
wouldn't take me any further – the same issues would still be there.
Some problems I bottled up; some I talked through with my wife;
but the best thing I did, which I know won't work for everyone, was
to design a website which portrayed the life I wanted to live as if it

were actually happening. Most happily, five years later, all of it has happened and more.

On the other hand, I do have friends who've had the most awful time with a severely brain-damaged child and a related court case going on for more than five years. Both parents are now off work, and he has been on some medication that has undoubtedly made a difference and just helped him to survive; and the truth is that I don't know how I'd cope in their situation.

I have chosen for your reading stories from people who have a positive and healing tale to tell, and I wish with all my heart that my daughter's had been one of them. Caitlin's tragedy aside, the truth is, and I have this on the highest authority, that 99 per cent of people like you and me who suffer crippling depression can and will recover. Depression is not a life sentence.

6

Feeling better: recovery positions

Think for yourself or someone else will.

(Anonymous)

The truth will set you free but first it will piss you off.

(Gloria Steinem, *Lifetime*,
television documentary, 4 December 1998)

We now need to move away from the medicalization of society, the belief that every problem requires a medical solution, and break the drug industry's stranglehold by insisting that our leaders treat public health separately from the commercial interests of the pharmaceutical industry.

(Phillip Knightley, February 2006)

Things to do to beat depression

Approaching the last fence with this book I was feeling quite overwhelmed by the quantity of writing on depression (most certainly not always quality). I was fortunate to come across a 97-page gem written by author and broadcaster Paul Vincent, *50 Things You Can Do Today to Beat Depression*. The book is calculated to be read in about an hour. The author's confidence and clarity are a breath of fresh air in the often muggy field of mental health writing. While giving someone a pill sends out a message that there is something wrong with us, Paul Vincent invites the reader to recognize that we are not sick but in need of some strong and useful 'exercises' for our situation.

For example: 'Depression is an overused word ... let's assume it is usually shorthand for "the problems we are facing", whatever those may be.' Or: 'Depression is a work of genius. It robs you of the very energy and hope that you need to cure it.' Or:

It is my belief that if you give this book an honest hour of your time, you can and will cure your depression for good ... You will need:

- an hour on your own;
- a pen;
- about fifteen pieces of blank paper;
- a clean empty litter bin (a cardboard box will do);
- a clock or watch;
- a mirror that is big enough to see your whole face;
- the TV definitely off, perhaps a CD player or iPod to hand, but turned off at this stage.

The author is certain that no single cure works on its own. For example, exercise is an excellent idea but by itself will not cure depression; and nor will diet, or talking, or taking drugs. Vincent's 50 individual exercises are wittily viewed as being each able to help by 2 per cent.

Paul Vincent periodically suffered depressive episodes which robbed him of his speaking voice, made him physically ill and hobbled his career as a writer. As he recovered, he set up a number of websites on the subject. He stressed that in the main he was a member of the public whose life had previously been ruled by depression. On the sites, he listed the measures that had helped him personally recover, and asked people to tell him what they found worked best, and how. Over 200,000 people hit the sites, and Vincent believes that it was far and away the best thing he has ever done in his life. He expected negative reactions from the medical fraternity but, surprisingly, all who contacted him were pleasant, and some clinics even wrote to say that they had copied the website exercises as handouts to patients. This was also my experience in consulting the experts, so three cheers to them.

I am grateful for Paul's permission to include a few summarized taster exercises to see if his approach is one you might find helpful.

2. LET'S DO SOMETHING
Read the next sentence very carefully.
DEPRESSION IS AN ILLNESS THAT ROBS PEOPLE OF THE BELIEF THAT THEY CAN CURE IT.
Right. Now cover that sentence with your hand and see if you can still remember it clearly.

Paul Vincent then promises to nag the reader, and asks us to read the capitalized sentence once more and then cover it up and see if we can remember it. After that, he asks us to clap our hands twice, for the simple reason that depression robs us of energy. And clap twice again. 'There is no doubt,' he continues, 'a very small percentage of people reading this will feel they were too cool or important to clap their hands.' He then tells us to sit up in our chairs and clap our hands again, twice, loudly.

Vincent suffered depression from about the age of 14. He does not inveigh against any method, including medication, which he tried. But what he does emphasize is this: 'NO **ONE** CURE WILL CHANGE MY LIFE 100%.' After all, the brain and our consciousness are much more intricate than, say, a broken bone, which takes several processes to enable healing.

'Depression is surprisingly complicated.' We then follow his repeat instructions to clap our hands loudly, twice, then repeat the sentence 'DEPRESSION IS AN ILLNESS THAT ROBS PEOPLE OF THE BELIEF THAT THEY CAN CURE IT', followed by the sentence 'NO **ONE** CURE WILL CHANGE MY LIFE 100%.' We are then invited to explore the 50 ways which can improve, even change, our lives by 2 per cent or more.

6. SEN-SAY-SHUN-ALL
You cannot beat depression with depression. Rig up some music you like, but something upbeat, maybe something with happy associations and memories. Play it in the background, or not, if you don't like music. Read the following list aloud:

- GLITTER
- SHINING
- HAPPY
- SUNSHINE
- RICH
- GOOD
- SENSATIONAL
- EXCITEMENT
- TREAT
- GOODIES
- SUCCESS
- HAPPINESS

- LAUGHTER
- PASSION
- FRESH
- FRUITFUL
- SMILE

Now read it again, this time smiling and with your eyes wide open and twinkling. With each word, still smiling, over-pronounce every syllable, e.g. SEN-SAY-SHUN-AL. This is based on research which shows that saying positive words helps a feeling of well-being. You can do this one as many times as you like. Nothing to lose, as it's free and easy.

10. PLAY TO YOUR STRENGTHS

Paul Vincent rightly refuses to ignore common sense, and I'm sure we can all affirm that common sense is often a rarity in our lives. Here, Paul suggests that we can reach a happier state by (1) reducing anxieties, for example, worries about the mortgage, passing exams, etc.; (2) always planning times in your weekly schedule for enjoyment; and (3) playing to your strengths.

29. WE ARE WHAT WE EAT ... and drink

We cannot, Vincent thinks, expect correct diet to cure depression on its own. He does, however, believe that excessive drinking and bad eating habits can cause or make depression worse. Bad eating and drinking is like 'fighting the battle with one hand tied behind your back ... And don't get me started on the subject of drugs ... dope doesn't just block brain receptors; it *kills off* entire neural pathways.' Have enough respect for alcohol and drugs to keep them your servant if you can.

32. GET READY TO HECKLE ...

The bit of advice that over the years created the biggest fuss for Paul Vincent was this: learn to love your own company. He believes that if you can learn to love your own company you can be free of depression: 'If you like yourself, if you don't compare yourself to others; if you are happy for others when they do well ... then you yourself will feel the happiest person alive.' Don't renounce your pals. Just try to learn to enjoy both friendship and being on your own as two separate and equal joys.

You bet! I feel great on antidepressants! Now when people get on my nerves, I just grab them round the throat and throw them against a wall. I tell you, hardly anyone has given me any hassle for weeks now!

34. LIFE IS NOT A BATTLE

Of all the suggestions in Vincent's tidy little book, this is the one which most closely resonated with my own and my acquaintances' experience of depression. So many people with depression seem to need to prove that we are 'worse' than others, that we are inconsolable and 'incurable'. Therefore we pooh-pooh any positive suggestions. I personally experienced this inconsolability factor after my daughter's death. 'When seeing life as a battle is destructive and time-consuming it may be better to not see situations as conflicts. In other words, only see a situation as a battle when it is in your *interests* to do so.' None of us chooses to be depressed, and our brain is where our thoughts are stored and processed; but we *can* choose what we think about all day. If we think happy thoughts all day we can become happy people. Let go of your battles. Choose happiness. It's worth a try.

43. TOMORROW AND FOR EVER

The essence of Paul Vincent's slim book (and the essence of this one too), is the power of our thoughts and putting these revised thoughts into action. We who have suffered or are now suffering depression tend to have a hard time accepting this notion. Why?

Because 'Depression is an illness that tries to rob you of the very skills and energies you need' to recover.

Placebo therapy

Placebos contain no active ingredients. Traditionally we call them sugar pills and they are always employed in clinical trials when trying to establish the safety and efficacy or otherwise of medications. In these trials one group is given the test drug and another group, acting as a means of comparison, is given a placebo. Double-blind trials are those in which neither the researcher nor the patient knows who receives the placebo and who receives the real drug.

The placebo effect shows what the mind and the body can achieve in the absence of a real drug but with the expectation of benefit. I have experienced the power of suggestion, first hand, albeit negatively. My mother died of Hodgkin's disease when I was six years old. I grew up convinced that I would also die at the same age as she did, which I thought was 33. By the time I reached 33, I was a married mother, writer and full-time teacher. One day I discovered swollen lymph glands under my arms, in my groin, in my neck. I rushed to the GP who made an *immediate* hospital appointment ... yes, dear reader, this was a few years ago. The consultant ran all the tests, and guess what? I was clear. I phoned my sister to tell her of my scare and my happy news, and said, 'What is so weird is that I've always thought I'd get cancer and die when I was 33, like Mum.' My sister paused. 'Linda, Mum wasn't 33 when she died; she was 41!'

Now, I know you can't cure or kill everything by the power of suggestion, and for years scientists have looked at the placebo effect as a figment of overactive patient imagination, probably well-deserved in my case. But positive claims for placebo power won't go away. Placebos have been especially helpful in recovering from depression. Studies in depressed people have found that almost as many are helped by placebo treatments as by active medications. One theory proposes that the brain makes more of its own pain-dousing opiates if the patient anticipates relief. Whatever the reason for the placebo effect, it reveals a resourcefulness and vast reservoir of healing power in the human body that is quite wondrous (Public Library of Science, <www.plos.org>; and see Lynch, 2004).

The placebo can work in active drugs for depression too. Basically the drug will work according to what the label says, what the doctor says, and what we want to believe. So, for example, the drug bupro-prion, or Zyban (UK) and Welbutrin (USA), is prescribed for giving up smoking and is also prescribed for depression. In other words, our minds and bodies will respond to what we are told a drug will do. When it's a sugar pill this seems to me OK. But when it's a powerful, expensive drug with side effects we are talking a different ball game.

Complementary and alternative therapies (CAT) include but are not limited to yoga, Chinese medicine, acupuncture, biofeedback, meditation, relaxation techniques, aromatherapy, massage, herbal treatments, t'ai chi, homeopathy, naturopathy, laughter therapy, music and dance therapy. The brief of this book is too modest to go into these therapies in a comprehensive way. There is no doubt that with a good practitioner these treatments can be healing and are safe. Take a good look and decide which one you think may be most helpful.

I want to devote a few words, however, to laugh out loud (lol) therapy, or laughter yoga as it is also called; it seems like such a lovely way to ease depression. Like so many truistic therapies, it is not new; remember our grandmothers saying that laughter is the best medicine? Laughter yoga is the brainchild of Dr Madan Kataria, a physician from Mumbai, India. He began the laughter club movement, which now has grown to in excess of 5,000 laughter clubs around the world. World Laughter Day took place in May 2006, with thousands of people attending laugh-ins (<www.laughteryoga.org>). Check it out.

Cognitive behavioural therapy

CBT is at present and for good reason 'flavour of the month' as a form of treating depression, although many counsellors are quite likely to be eclectic in their practice of listening and healing. I am giving it extensive space in this chapter because I'd like you to have a good introduction. Like any treatment, CBT is imperfect. It depends hugely on the practitioner's competence and won't suit everyone. The term 'cognition' means thinking, 'the mental act or process by which knowledge is acquired'.

CBT treats how we think about ourselves, about the world around us, and about other people in our world. And importantly it is concerned with exploring how what we do affects our thoughts and our feelings.

Successful treatment with CBT can help us change how we think, i.e. the 'cognitive' bit, and also help change what we do, i.e. our behaviour. Rightly appropriated, the changes we make can help us to feel better. Another interesting aspect of CBT which is unlike many therapeutic styles is that it concentrates on the here and now, problems which plague our present – rather than focusing on our past, as in, for example, 'I am insecure because my mother died when I was six.' CBT seeks out ways to help our present state of mind.

Proponents of CBT claim its success in treating many distressing states, including anxiety, depression, panic, phobias including agoraphobia and social phobias, bulimia, obsessive compulsive disorder and post-traumatic stress disorder.

CBT can help make sense of life difficulties and suffering, by placing the problem or situation in smaller 'portions', thus helping us to see how each issue is connected and what it is doing to us as a result.

How CBT works

A problem or situation might be the loss of a loved one, or the loss of a job. From this difficult time follow thoughts, emotions, physical issues and actions. It may seem obvious to state that all these reactions are interconnected, i.e. how we think about a problem affects how we feel physically and emotionally. It can also alter what you do about it.

There are better and worse ways of responding to most situations, depending on the way we think about them. Let's say I've had a lousy day and feel very low. I decide to get some fresh air and take the dogs for a walk. Someone I know and like, a new acquaintance perhaps, walks by on the other side of the road and ignores me. I might respond to this by thinking the worst: they ignored me, so they must dislike me. On the other hand, I might think, gosh, they look a bit preoccupied. I wonder if they are OK.

My emotions might include additional sadness and rejection because I've been ignored. On the other hand I might be concerned for them.

Physically I might feel tummy ache, fatigue, even slightly ill. On the other hand I might feel comfortable that I had not presumed their dislike.

What do I do about it? I could go home and stay away from them. On the other hand I could give them a ring and check that they are OK. The same state of affairs has led to very different outcomes, and this depended totally on how I thought about the situation. Think/feel/do. If I jumped to the first conclusion without, let's face it, any proper evidence, it may result in uncomfortable feelings and negative actions.

Knowing me I'd probably dwell on a patently minor incident and feel worse as a result. But if I ring the other person, overcoming my dislike of the telephone, there's a good chance I'll feel better about myself. If I don't, I won't have the chance to correct any of my possible misunderstandings about what they think of me – and I know I'd feel worse.

Another quirky but vivid example: three blind people enter a room and encounter an elephant for the first time. One inspects the trunk and concludes the creature is a snake. The second finds a leg and decides this thing is a tree. The third finds the tail and is convinced she's found a rope.

To point out the obvious, each blind person has a different perspective. Translating the parable, we all have not only different but very limited perspectives and none of us can see the whole picture. This is where other insights come in; if we can see more of the picture then we can think differently and begin to perceive 'the elephant in the room'.

Any 'vicious cycle' of negative thoughts can make us feel worse. We might even start to believe quite unrealistic (and unpleasant) things about ourselves. This is because when we are upset, we are more likely to jump to conclusions and to interpret things in extreme and unhelpful ways. Well, I know this pattern fits me to a tee.

Successful counselling with CBT can help break the cycle of altered thinking, feelings and behaviour. Clarity and insight can help us change the sequence – a kind of 'do-it-yourself' process of problem-solving.

Other life issues such as debt, employment and housing difficulties are also important. If I can improve one area, I am quite likely to improve other parts of my life as well.

What CBT involves

CBT sessions vary, and can involve individual or group work. Some people do well with a self-help book or working online. If you are able to choose individual therapy, you will usually meet with a therapist for several weekly or fortnightly sessions. Each meeting lasts between 30 and 60 minutes. In the initial meetings, your counsellor will discuss the treatment and whether or not it will be useful to you.

Although CBT does emphasize the present, your counsellor will quite likely also ask questions about your background and your earlier years. Sometimes it helps to talk about the past in order to understand how it impinges on life in the present. The decision is yours as to what you want to deal with in the immediate, medium and long-term future.

With your counsellor you divide each problem into its separate components. Your counsellor may suggest you keep a diary in order to identify your way of thinking, your emotional patterns, physical feelings and your actions. Are they unrealistic or unhelpful? How do they affect one another, and how do they affect you? Then your counsellor will help you work out how to change unhelpful thoughts or patterns of behaviour. This is, of course, more difficult than it sounds.

When you find out what you can change, you may get some 'homework' from your counsellor in order to practise these changes in real-life situations. For example, you might replace a negative and possibly self-critical thought with a more realistic thought developed with the help of your counsellor. You might realize that you are about to do something unwise and instead do something smart. At the following meeting you talk about how you have managed since the previous session. You can then weed out the 'homework' tasks which seemed either too difficult or not helpful. It is up to you, and you do not have to continue doing what you feel uncomfortable doing.

One advantage of CBT is that the skills you learn can be continued after the counselling sessions have ended, making it likely that you will recover and deal with your problems effectively.

How effective is CBT?

CBT is one of the most effective treatments for conditions where anxiety or depression is the main problem, and appears to be the most effective psychological treatment for moderate and severe depression. It is more effective than antidepressants for many types of depression.

CBT is used in many conditions, including the most common problems – anxiety and depression. However, it isn't for everyone and another type of talking treatment may work better for you. CBT is undoubtedly a better option than medication; neither antidepressants nor tranquillizers should be used as long-term treatments for anxiety or depression.

Problems with CBT

If you are feeling low and are having difficulty concentrating, it can be hard, at first, to 'gel' with CBT – or, indeed, any psychotherapy. This may make you feel disappointed or overwhelmed. A good therapist will pace your sessions so you can cope with the work you are trying to do. It can also sometimes be difficult to talk about feelings of depression, anxiety, shame or anger.

How long will the treatment last?

A course of CBT sessions may last from six weeks to six months. It will depend on the type of problem and how the therapy is working for you. The availability of CBT varies between different areas and there may be a waiting list for treatment.

What if the symptoms come back?

Although you will hopefully have the necessary skills to deal with future situations, there is always a possibility that the anxiety or depression will return. If this happens, your CBT skills should make it easier for you to control them. So, it is important to keep practising your CBT skills, even after you are feeling better.

Is CBT for you?

Depression and anxiety are unpleasant. They can seriously affect your ability to work and enjoy life. CBT can help you to control the symptoms. It is unlikely to have a negative effect on your life, apart from the time you need to devote to it.

If you are in doubt, discuss the alternatives with your doctor. Try to read up about alternative therapies. If you want to 'try before you buy', get hold of a self-help book or CD-ROM to see what makes sense to you. You could always wait to see if you get better anyway – if you change your mind later, ask to be referred for CBT when you are ready to try it.

The following letter was printed in the *Guardian Weekly* (July 2006) in response to an article advocating CBT:

I have lived with depression and anxiety for more than half a century and not found them amenable to piecemeal solutions such as CBT ... It is as presumptive for outside experts and specialists to impose their solutions on depression as it is for some nations to foist democracy on others. What this culture calls 'mental illness' isn't a single, simple state but a whole ecology – labyrinthine, dendritic [branching like a tree], multi-faceted, endlessly dying and being reborn.

CBT is useful in beginning negotiations with the 'inner terrorists' who stalk the psyche. It can help modulate and recode malignant self-talk by challenging and changing the underlying belief patterns. But in and of itself it's not enough. I have found it helpful in conjunction with acupuncture, Reiki, spiritual practice, dance, dreams, breath-work, rest and relax-ation, making music, making love, mindful eating, gardening, walking – all in a context of rigorous self-transformation, of exploring without shame or denial this particular way of being human, and of learning to love neighbour, self and planet. Solutions, whether to mental illness, climate change or fundamentalism, must be as intricate, fluid and robust as the issues.

Other psychological therapies

Your head may be swimming by now with too much information. The following list of brief summaries, which is not by any means exhaustive, is intended to give you an idea of the variety of therapies available, should you decide that you want to talk with someone to heal your depression.

Psychoanalysis

As developed by Sigmund Freud, psychoanalysis usually requires several therapy sessions per week over an extensive period of time. The basis of this therapy is that our existing psychological problems result from repressed memories and feelings from our past. These repressed memories reside in our unconscious mind and create emotional difficulties when they surface in our conscious life. Psychoanalysis is more commonly used if there is a long history of depression or anxiety and the causes are not readily apparent. Unlike CBT, where the emphasis is on the present, patients are encouraged to talk freely about the past, including painful experiences and emotions. Newer psychoanalytic therapies are less time-consuming than what is called classic Freudian analysis.

Behavioural therapies

These therapies work with us to change patterns of behaviour directly. They are an outgrowth of behaviourism, which contends that our behaviours, emotions, moods and responses are both conditioned and learned. The classic example is Pavlov's dog, which salivated when a dinner bell rang. We can 'unlearn' what we have 'learned' as well, and our 'conditioned responses' can be 're-conditioned'. Destructive behaviour patterns, both physiological (as in drug addiction) and psychological (as, for example, verbal abuse) can be 're-conditioned'. Behaviours central to a lifestyle may be difficult to change, but behaviour therapy focuses on unlearning old negative and dysfunctional behaviours and learning new and healthier ones. It is thought that people can act their way into new ways of thinking, as opposed to thinking their way into new ways of acting; new behaviours can lead to new and healthier emotions. Working on destructive behaviours can help depression.

Behavioural psychotherapy is particularly effective for anxiety, panic, phobias, obsessive compulsive problems and various kinds of social or sexual difficulty. Relief from symptoms often occurs quite quickly.

Family and marital therapy

This is a group therapy which concentrates on the family and individuals within it and often involves two therapists. People's problems are often not theirs alone, but the result of relationship problems in a marriage, partnership or family. When one member of a family has problems, it creates problems within the family unit. Family therapy can be very useful with the following issues:

• Discovering whether one family member is carrying an excessive emotional burden for the entire family.
• Helping family members appreciate both our individuality and our importance in the family unit.
• Defining boundaries between family members, clarifying roles and functions, and allowing all members to realize their full possibilities.
• Solving power imbalances and establishing boundaries if one family member is a 'control freak'.

Group therapy

Several people with similar sorts of problems meet regularly with one or more therapists. These sessions may be longer than in individual psychotherapy. Group therapy may appear less intimate, but it is not a cheap or second-rate treatment – it is in fact the best treatment for some problems. If the group is gathered around a certain issue (depression, alcoholism, compulsive gambling), it can be a powerful support. Prejudice, stigma, fear and shame can transform into their positive counterparts. The experience of discovering that you are not alone, and of being able to help other people, is powerfully encouraging and is often the first step towards getting better.

Interpersonal therapies

The notion on which these therapies are based is that depression can often be worsened by problems between ourselves and others in social relationships. Unhappiness in relationships and the emotional stresses which inevitably attend them are dealt with. As in CBT, it is the present more than the past to which the therapies are directed. Interpersonal therapy aims to deal with symptoms in a relatively short period. The therapist helps to develop coping mechanisms and social skills, to strengthen family ties, friendships and working relationships. If this therapy is for you, you will be helped to gain skills in defusing confrontational situations, with practical advice on what to say, and what to do.

Pastoral counselling

Pastoral counselling is specialized in that it is the realm of ordained clergy trained in pastoral psychotherapy. It is unique in that it combines the healing resources of the Judeo-Christian tradition with modern psychotherapeutic methods. The many issues which converge in mental health and religious sensibilities can be explored. However, just as there can be good and bad doctors and therapists, there can be good and bad pastoral counsellors. Good pastoral counsellors should be able to provide healing resources and a profound sense of hope. Bad counsellors can increase anxiety, create dependency and block the journey to wholeness. For information on pastoral counselling, visit <www.instituteofcounselling.org.uk> (BACP approved).

Client-centred therapy

This therapy is often referred to as Rogerian, after its founder, Carl Rogers. Rogers was a pioneer in person-centred counselling. He taught that lasting and true change in our lives comes about through 'experience in a relationship'. The therapist builds a relationship of respect and understanding and is non-directive: the therapist doesn't interpret psychological events or emotions or advise a certain action, but helps to clarify feelings and thoughts and promote self-esteem. Positive regard is a hallmark of this approach. Should this not be true of all therapies?

Finding a therapist

A psychotherapist may be a psychiatrist, psychologist or other mental health professional who has had further specialist training in psychotherapy. Increasingly there are a number of psychotherapists who do not have a background as psychiatrists, psychologists or social workers, but have an in-depth training in psychotherapy.

Ask your GP or an alternative medicine practitioner, who will be able to refer you to a qualified person in your area. It is important that a psychotherapist has a recognized qualification and your GP should ensure that this is the case before making a referral. As in so many fields there are charlatans as well as the 'real McCoy'. Don't be afraid to 'shop around' for someone who suits your needs.

Medication-free treatment for psychological distress

In my research I discovered a very interesting and encouraging service for depressed and distressed people. Dr Toby Tyler Watson is executive director of Associated Psychological Health Services in Wisconsin, USA (the website is listed in Useful Addresses at the back of this book). He directs an intensive day and outpatient clinic specializing in medication-free treatment. I am grateful for permission to quote from his website.

A person suffering from psychological or behavioral problems has been emotionally wounded or violated. *It is possible to hide emotional wounds through drugs, electrical shock and other 'technologies'.* True healing, however, comes from restoring and renewing the things that define and reflect our humanity. Things like intimacy, community, art, music, spirituality and play. We address all these dimensions that make us fully human: emotional, psychological, physical, social and spiritual. This is where healing and self-empowerment truly begins ...

We are a community-based psychological treatment center offering a broad range of psychological services including a comprehensive three hour per day and five hour per day enhanced group treatment program, featuring traditional and innovative individual and group therapies. Our specialized program offers an alternative to de-humanizing and coercive institutions that are ineffective in eliminating the problems over the lifespan. Treatment programs and services are designed to positively impact the full spectrum of emotional, psychological, physical, social and spiritual dimensions that make us fully human. Our treatment facility is one of only a few of its kind in the world that is dedicated to and specializes in treatment of psychological, emotional and behavioral problems without the use of psychiatric drugs. Associated Psychological Health Services is also one of the only treatment centers supporting a patient's choice to lower and eliminate their use of and/or need for drugs.

Drug free? First, let me start out by stating that I am not anti-drugs. Everyday we take drugs such as caffeine (e.g. coffee or soda throughout the day to perk us up) and depressants (e.g. wine at dinner to soothe and calm us down from our hectic day). However, no one pretends or informs us that we have a caffeine or dopamine deficiency when we are groggy in the morning or because the drug changes our behavior and feelings. No one tells us we have a genetic chemical imbalance because we look horrible when we stop the coffee or go without it. Drugs serve a purpose and have a definite effect upon our brain, thus, psychiatric drugs also cause changes in brain chemistry, attitudes, behaviors, thoughts and feelings. Sometimes the behavioral, emotional or psychological effects are desired; often they are not (i.e. adverse side effects).

I was trained as a scientist-practitioner. My understanding and thought processes are based both in science, through my formal training, and in my humanity (i.e. in my spirituality-life lessons). Initially during my psychological training, I did not believe people suffering from such things often labeled Schizophrenia, Bipolar, ADD/ADHD, etc. could be helped without the use of psychotropic drugs. I was told early on these people had brain diseases and their suffering was not the result of a magnitude of social factors within the environment. Often (I was told) it was a combination of environment and underlying illness waiting to be activated. Later during my graduate studies ... I was enlightened.

I have now been treating people often diagnosed Manic Depressive (Bipolar) and Major Depressive Disorder Severe without ANY medications, AND without the negative consequences often reported by medical model treatment centers and supporters. This is in spite of not using drugs, locks, force and intrusive measures to keep the peace and/or symptoms at bay. There are no locks on our doors, no coercive techniques or agendas. While in treatment, there have not been any major acts of violence or suicides either, despite unfounded warnings verbalized to me during my graduate training (i.e. if you stop taking your drugs you will not be able to control your homicidal, suicidal or psychotic thoughts). I have been successfully treating people, not diagnosis, for many years, and I have honored the patient's right not to use or rely upon medications ...

There are a significant portion of consumers of mental health services who either do not benefit from psychotropic medications, who are allergic to such drugs and/or who are simply intolerant of such drugs. These people require alternative treatments which are not biological in nature. There are only a few facilities in the world which offer pure psycho-social solutions on an exclusive basis in an enhanced group treatment format. Patients have the right to determine the process and modality of their treatment ... at APHS they are active participants in their own recovery, irrespective of severity of symptoms or prior diagnostic labels.

It's elementary ...

7

Faith as a recovery position

The physical, psychological, and social dimensions of depression come together in the spiritual dimension, which is where our humanity finds meaning and purpose in life.'

(Hunter and Hunter, 2004)

This discussion could logically be integrated in the previous chapter, but I want to set the faith issue apart because I've discovered somewhat to my surprise that raising the question of faith in a book on depression appears to be a risky business. Not necessarily a bad thing, of course. To me, it is self-evident that we humans are mind-body-spirit organisms, more than the sum of our parts. Relax, though, because I'm not going to try to convert you; I am hoping to reach an understanding that the faith factor as I understand it can help in recovering from depression, especially 'in our times'. I accept, however, that readers will have different definitions of faith, some seeing it only in a religious context (and any number of varieties within that broad sweep); others will have humanist concepts of faith, and some of you will not find it a helpful word at all. I can only write on this most personal of subjects from my own perspective and my hope is that if you stick with this chapter you might find something thought-provoking and perhaps of use.

If you choose to read on, you will need to know that when I talk about faith I am not talking about dogmatic belief systems or fundamentalist doctrines. My 'faith' is always striving to be open, to understand, to admit doubt and uncertainty as an essential part of growth and development. That is why it cannot be dogmatic; it is a living, growing and changing aspect of my life.

Let's talk about one of my favourite subjects for a minute: me! I have a faith, and it colours everything I see. What do I mean when I use this word? It is primarily a way of seeing. For me it is visual, and it comes in colour. Possibly this is partly because I recall asking my mum when I was about four years old, 'Are there more colours in the world than I can see now?' 'There sure are, honey,' she said, 'and never stop looking.' It was evening and the stars were coming out. 'Have you ever noticed how many colours there are in darkness?' she said. Then she named some of them for me – lightning blue and gold and silver – and I envisioned them as holes of light peeping through a tie-dyed sky-blanket of purples and aubergine and cerulean and almost black. Keep looking for colours. The personal language of my faith comes from my Judeo-Christian roots, and from the teachings of Jesus, but it is not exclusive or dismissive of other roots and ideas. What holds it together is love, what drives it is hope.

When I look at someone I see a rainbow person of mind, body and spirit. I cannot see your mind or your spirit any more than I can see the wind or love – I can only see the fruits of these invisible presences. My faith tells me what I cannot prove, but absence of proof is not proof of absence and, further, I believe that the God I worship loves each one of us and has placed room for her/him/ itself in your being. I don't know where that being (soul is as good a word as any) is located. I think it permeates everything as well as transcending it.

This faith of mine doesn't always help me. For example, when my daughter hanged herself I, like any parent who loves their children (and I qualify this now only because when I wrote my last book I discovered to my deep shock that not all parents love their children), was cast into an inner darkness defying description. My faith didn't help, even enough to quote the words of Christ on the cross, 'My God, my God, why have you forsaken me?'

This, I believe, is the nature of deep grief, which experts will tell you is similar to but not the same as depression. Which doesn't mean that grieving people don't ever get depressed. But what made me inconsolable and uncomforted by my faith was the very primitive sense of loss, of the Caitlin-shaped maelstrom in my life that can't be filled with faith or lovers or God or food or work or anything. She was never going to run through the door and say, 'Hey Mum, I'm home!' or complain about the washing up after meals when it was her turn. She is not here, getting her degree and thriving in her chosen profession and marrying and maybe having kids. Her body lies buried in a beautiful local churchyard, where birth and death (we existed!) are remembered with flowers and pebbles and trinkets. And that is partly what dead means.

But to me that is not all that dead means. I believe that when she died her soul, if you will, became part of a wondrous and mysterious cosmic intelligence that I cannot begin to understand. It is a place of radiance and learning and galactic growth. We will be reunited too. I could go on for hours about my view of life both before (read 'this life') and after death, of that John Lennon lyric (my version goes, 'imagine there's a heaven').

I cannot prove to you this faith any more than you can prove to me your faith or 'no faith' position. What *is* true is that what we think about death is vitally important, especially when we are depressed.

About a year ago (it was seven years after Caitlin's death) the grief made a tectonic shift. I began to feel different, that it was important to attend to the living, to give my long-suffering and heroic life partner the support so richly deserved and deserving – to have fun and rejoice again, because Caitlin was, for want of a better word – settled. I attributed this growing awareness mostly to my partner; saying that she looked after me does not begin to describe what she was for me. Letting go is the wrong term. So is moving on. It's more like a progressive emergence from under an avalanche, gradually seeing and then allowing the light, of life itself, for oneself and for the people one loves, to soak into our being, to refocus on the living, the present and on the translucent and terrible beauty of the years gifted to us. I guess this is where faith for me comes in big-time.

I do not, however, mean to imply that healing from depression is only available to those who believe in a continuation in some form of life after physical death. Many atheists believe that we can learn to accept our own death as part of the story of life, and even welcome it as the appropriate end to a long life. Perhaps this doesn't help with the grief of a premature death but people who don't share my faith do find ways to cope.

When you are depressed you will need to be able to talk about so many things: life as it is, how you feel physically, issues of

self-worth and confidence, how you perceive work and relationships, how to find freedom and to move, perhaps painfully slowly, from despair to recovery. If you or I are depressed and talking to a counsellor (hopefully a competent, respectful, empathetic and no-nonsense counsellor with a strong built-in crap detector), we will need to discuss how we feel about our own death. Here's one of the things Dorothy Rowe has to say about the big D (for which read 'death' or 'depression' interchangeably, or both):

> British people are not great church-goers when compared to people in some other countries, but whenever surveys are taken of religious beliefs a large percentage of British people say that they believe in God and an afterlife. Similar surveys in the USA give even higher percentages of believers. Such percentages would seem to suggest that religious beliefs are normal and important ... [But] whenever I ask a group of clinical psychologists whether they believe in an afterlife most of them say they do not, and when I advise them that in therapy with a depressed person it is a good idea to discover what that person's religious beliefs are, many of my colleagues look at me strangely and think that I have ceased to be a rational person, having discovered religion in my old age.

> (Rowe, 2001)

Dorothy Rowe asked her clients what they think their own death means to them:

> There are only two possibilities. Either death is the end of my identity or it is a doorway to another life ... We all know whether we see our identity vanishing with our death or our identity in some form passing to another life, since it is this choice which has determined what we see as the purpose of our life. If we see death as the end of our identity then we have the task of making this, our only life, in some way satisfactory; if we see our death as a doorway to another life then we have the task of trying to live this life according to the rules of entry to the next life.

Rowe continues by pointing out that we may choose different rules, but we all have them, however unexplored they may be.

So how we feel about our own death is important. Not just our depression after the loss of loved ones (for example: 'My mother died when I was six. I heard my gran say that my mother had been ill ever since I was born and I still feel it was my fault') but our faith or religious beliefs and how they work.

I was born and grew up in America, a great church-going nation, with a massive percentage believing in an afterlife, and have as an adult chosen to live in England. British people may not be great church-goers, but a large percentage believe in God and also in an afterlife. These statistics normalize religious beliefs. Therefore it is a problem when many in charge of our mental well-being and the treatment of our depression think that faith is at best credulous, stupid, neurotic or at worst psychotic. Some psychologists are so opposed to religious faith that they have no respect for the faith of other people. I agree with Dorothy Rowe that any therapist or psychiatrist worth their salt needs to respect the thoughts we have about faith, life and death.

Still, many psychologists justify their antipathy towards faith issues with the blunt observation that psychology is a science and science is opposed to religion. From my perspective, the cracks in this attitude are huge – there are some human experiments not reducible to the rigours of the scientific method for starters. They are the wiggly evasive things of life. The stuff of faith and feelings.

Our legacy in the West, largely the reductionist approach of the scientific method, thankfully has shown signs of development in my lifetime. For instance, many psychiatrists are concerned about the loss of the soul of their profession, by which I mean the emphasis on drugs and physical interventions which has led to a neglect of the person being treated and her/his life experiences. 'Patients are fit into the Procrustean bed of a diagnosis based on the most recent edition of *DSM-IV* [*The Diagnostic and Statistical Manual of Mental Disorders*, see Chapter 4]. Treatments prescribed are frequently cookbook, with a pharmacologic recipe for virtually every problem' (Blazer, in Stannard, 2000).

Some of the most vocal criticism of trends in biological psychiatry has come from the psychoanalytic tradition. Psychiatrists need to listen more and medicate less, they say. There is even an interest in the spiritual. Freud stated that the possession of religious beliefs was evidence of a neurosis and that religion was a universal neurosis. And although Carl Jung opposed this view it was Freud who most influenced British psychiatry.

It's most interesting to speculate what Freud would think of this trend, since to my knowledge he never gave up on his belief in the biological basis for understanding and treating emotional suffering, and believed that the body and soul were one biological organ.

This renewed interest in questions of faith and in the spiritual is opening a dialogue between psychiatry and religion. An important bridge between these unlikely allies is our stories of emotional distress. So there is reason to hope for what Dorothy Rowe so eloquently speaks: rather than challenging or belittling the faith of their patients, psychiatrists may begin to call upon the resources for healing inherent in the stories.

None of us lives solely by rational thought. Some things will be, must be, taken on trust. A person's belief that life ends in death is an act of faith just as surely as is the belief that death is a doorway to eternal life. Those of us who learn to cope as we recover from depression will hold to a faith or belief system which is optimistic and even courageous, regardless of what we think happens after our death. Those of us who do not cope will hold to a faith or belief which serves to ensnare us in hopelessness. Remember Paul

Vincent: 'Depression is a work of genius. It robs you of the very energy and hope that you need to cure it.'

One great and untapped strength of Eastern mysticism is a core notion of the indivisibility of mind, body and spirit. In the West we tend to be trained in the dialectic: we categorize things, dividing human nature into physical *or* spiritual, body *or* soul, biological *or* psychological, nature *or* nurture, secular *or* religious, personal *or* social (Hunter and Hunter, 2004). People of faith tend to lodge our religious faith in an Infinite Absolute transcendent Being, an uncreated creator. The trouble with these categories is that they get in the way of our seeing the whole picture. The reality is interconnectedness. Humpty Dumpty ends up in component parts when he falls, but we need to have all the pieces to put him together again. And where depression is concerned, we can no more locate a 'depression organ' than we can locate a human soul organ or find a place in the brain that likes cauliflower better than cabbage. A letter from a blogging Buddhist friend whose cartoons grace this book has an interesting perspective and I've included some extracts below which might be helpful in thinking about the role and nature of faith:

Dear Linda

There are millions of Buddhists who'd agree with your position on the importance of spiritual development and of faith in overcoming depression, but who'd disagree entirely that this could be defined under the blanket term of God.

There are many Buddhists in the world who don't even believe in the notion of a 'Higher Power' or 'Creator', believing as we do that this 'higher power' is no higher than ourselves and what we can achieve by revealing our Buddha nature in everyday life.

In Buddhism there is no such thing as superior beings, other than what we consider to be superior or inferior teachings, according to the wisdom and enlightenment that they impart – or superior or inferior behaviour, I suppose one could say too ...

I can say without a doubt, that practising Buddhism has relieved me of depression. Buddhism also teaches the importance of wisdom in daily life (including respecting our bodies), as well as of taking action to improve one's life and also help others.

Our practice is totally based in being active within society, not in going off on retreat from the world ...

I do believe that faith is essential, and that depression is a spiritual problem, but I also believe that in modern society our physical health has been compromised and we are under attack to the point of having damaged immune systems that make us very vulnerable to a huge amount of physical illnesses.

So my friend Emma sees her faith as taking responsibility for herself and a better world. Faith is a way of seeing. Depression is so vicious because it convinces us that 'This will not end. I will never get better.' In the treatment of depression, the areas of spiritual mental and physical health must be integrated. Physical, psychic, spiritual and cultural conditions can distort our sense of wholeness and well-being. Freedom from distress is when the entire human person, body, mind and spirit, as individuals and in relationships reaches a state of well-being. Bondage to distress occurs when the delicate balance in the human person has changed for the worse and there is no longer a sense of well-being. Release from this bondage can come in many forms.

William Sloane Coffin is one of my high-school heroes. He died in April 2006 at the age of 81. For years he served as chaplain of Yale University, counselling and inspiring thousands of his students. He was a master of what we today call 'the soundbite'. I treasure many things he had to say but one will stay with me always. One of his students, who incidentally suffered from crippling depression, challenged Coffin's faith stance, saying, 'Faith is just a crutch.' Coffin replied, 'What makes you think you don't limp?'

Ten days after his son, Alex, was killed in a car accident in 1983, William Sloane Coffin delivered a powerful sermon to his congregation at Riverside Church in New York City. Although directly addressing his bereavement, he explained in no uncertain terms how he was helped to live beyond a loss which can cripple for life, just as depression can cripple. Yet he described being caught and rescued by love and by faith. He quoted from the end of Hemingway's *A Farewell to Arms*: 'The world breaks everyone, then some become strong at the broken places.' And, referring to the many messages of love and support he had received he said, 'My own broken heart is mending, and largely thanks to so many of you … for if in the last week I have relearned one lesson, it is that love not only begets love, it transmits strength.'

Whatever your faith, dear reader, I hope you can say 'Amen' to that.

Appendix 1

Withdrawal protocols for SSRI antidepressants

SSRI stands for selective serotonin reuptake inhibitor. This does not mean that these drugs are selective to the serotonin system or that they are in some sense pharmacologically 'clean'. It means they have little effects on the norepinephrine/noradrenaline system.

There are seven SSRIs on the market:

> citalopram (Cipramil UK, Celexa USA)
> escitalopram (Lexapro)
> fluoxetine (Prozac)
> fluvoxamine (Faverin UK, Luvox USA)
> paroxetine (Seroxat UK, Paxil USA)
> sertraline (Lustral UK, Zoloft USA)
> venlafaxine (Efexor)

Venlafaxine in doses up to 150 mg is an SSRI. Over 150 mg it also inhibits noradrenaline reuptake.

Withdrawal symptoms

SSRI withdrawal symptoms break down into two groups. The first group may be unlike anything you have had before, for instance dizziness ('When I turn to look at something I feel my head lags behind') or 'electric head', which includes a number of strange brain sensations ('It's almost like the brain is having a version of goose pimples'). You may experience any of the following:

- electric shock-like sensations – 'zaps'
- other strange tingling or painful sensations
- nausea, diarrhoea, flatulence
- headache
- muscle spasms/tremor

- dreams, including agitated dreams or other vivid dreams
- agitation
- hallucinations or other visual or auditory disturbances

The second group are symptoms which may lead you or your physician to think that all you have are features of your original problem. These include:

- depression and anxiety – probably the commonest two symptoms
- labile mood – emotions swinging wildly
- irritability
- confusion
- fatigue/malaise – flu-like feelings
- insomnia or drowsiness
- sweating
- feelings of unreality
- feelings of being hot or cold
- change of personality

Is this withdrawal?

There are three ways to distinguish SSRI withdrawal from the nervous problems that the SSRI might have been used to treat in the first instance.

First, if the problem begins immediately on reducing or halting a dose or begins within hours or days or perhaps even weeks of so doing then it is more likely to be a withdrawal problem. If the original problem has been treated and you are doing well, then on discontinuing treatment no new problems should show up for several months or indeed several years.

Second, if the nervousness or other odd feelings that appear on reducing or halting the SSRI (sometimes after just missing a single dose) clear up when you are put back on the SSRI or the dose is put back up, then this also points towards a withdrawal problem rather than a return of the original illness. When original illnesses return, they take a long time to respond to treatment. The relatively immediate response of symptoms on discontinuation to the reinstitution of treatment points towards a withdrawal problem.

Third, the features of withdrawal may overlap with features of the nervous problem for which you were first treated – both may contain elements of anxiety and of depression. However, withdrawal will also often contain new features not in the original state, such as pins and needles, tingling sensations, electric shock sensations, pain and a general flu-like feeling.

It should be noted that many people will have no problems on withdrawing. Some will have minimal problems, which may peak after a few days before diminishing. Symptoms can remain for some weeks or months. Others will have greater problems, which can be helped by the management plan outlined below.

However, there will be a group of people who are simply unable to stop whatever approach they take. Others will be able to stop but will find problems persisting for months or years afterwards. It is important to recognize this latter possibility in order to avoid punishing yourself. Specialist help may make a difference for some people in these two groups, if only to provide possible antidotes to attenuate the problems of ongoing SSRIs such as loss of libido.

How to withdraw

If there are any hints of problems on withdrawal from SSRIs, the management of withdrawal is something to be done in consultation with your physician. You may wish to show this to your GP. Over-rapid withdrawal may even be medically hazardous, particularly in older persons.

1 (a) Convert the dose of SSRI you are on to an equivalent dose of Prozac liquid. Seroxat/Paxil 20 mg, Efexor 75 mg, Cipramil/Celexa 20 mg, Lustral/Zoloft 50 mg are equivalent to 20 mg of Prozac liquid. Or 40 mg Seroxat/Paxil to 40 mg Prozac. The rationale for this is that Prozac has a very long half-life, which helps to minimize withdrawal problems.

The liquid form permits the dose to be reduced more slowly than can be done with pills. Some people may become agitated on switching from Seroxat/Paxil to Prozac, in which case one option is take a short course of diazepam until this settles down.

1 (b) A further option is to convert to a liquid form of whatever drug you are on. Many people cannot change easily from Seroxat/Paxil tablets to Prozac liquid and switching to Seroxat/Paxil liquid may do the trick instead.

1 (c) An alternative is to change to the tricyclic clomipramine (Anafranil) 100 mg per day. This comes in 25 mg and 10 mg capsules, permitting a more gradual dose reduction than with other SSRIs. The 10 mg capsules can be opened up and part of the contents emptied out, permitting an even more gradual lowering of the dose.

2 In all cases stabilize on one of these options for up to four weeks before proceeding further.

3 For uncomplicated withdrawal, it may be possible to then drop the dose by a quarter.

4 If there has been no problem with step 2, a week or two later the dose can be reduced to half of the original. Alternatively if there has been a problem with the original drop, the dose should be reduced by 1 mg amounts in weekly or two-weekly decrements.

5 From a dose of Prozac 10 mg liquid or Anafranil 10 mg, consider reducing by 1 mg every few days over the course of several weeks – or months if need be. With Prozac liquid this can be done by dilution.

6 If there are difficulties at any particular stage the answer is to wait at that stage for a longer period of time before reducing further.

7 If there were problems switching to Prozac at a 20 mg level, it might be possible to do so when the dose of Seroxat/Paxil reduces to the 10 mg level.

Complexities of withdrawal

Some people are extremely sensitive to withdrawal effects. If there are problems with step 1 above, return to the original dose and from there reduce by 1 mg steps per week or as tolerated.

Withdrawal and dependence are physical phenomena. But some people can get understandably phobic about withdrawal particularly if the experience is literally shocking. If you think you have become phobic, a clinical psychologist or nurse therapist may be able to help manage the phobic problem.

Self-help support groups can be invaluable. Join one. If there is none nearby, consider setting one up. There will be lots of others with a similar problem.

There are some grounds to believe that another option is to substitute St John's Wort for the SSRI. If a dose of three tablets of St John's Wort is tolerated instead of the SSRI, this can then be reduced slowly – by one pill per fortnight or even per month or by halving tablets.

Some people for understandable reasons may prefer this approach. But it needs to be noted that St John's Wort has its own set of inter-actions with other pills and its own problems and you may wish to consult your physician if this is the option you choose.

There are likely to be dietary factors that may help or hinder. Some SSRIs affect blood sugar levels, others raise blood lipid levels. This may explain why snacking or grazing seems to be useful for some patients, and taking sugary drinks useful for others. Caffeine or any other foods that can make you more nervous or stimulated should be avoided during this period.

Follow-up

The problems posed by withdrawal may stabilize to the point where you can get on with life. But whether it is or is not possible to withdraw, it is important to note ongoing problems and to get your doctor or someone to report them if possible to the appropriate bodies – such as the Commission on Human Medicines, part of the MHRA. New health problems such as diabetes or raised blood lipid levels may have a link to prior or ongoing treatment.

There are clear effects on the heart from SSRIs and from some there are likely to be cardiac problems during the post-withdrawal period. Such problems if they occur should be noted and recorded.

SSRIs are well known to impair sexual functioning. The conven-tional view has been that once the drug is stopped, functioning comes back to normal. There are indicators, however, that this may not be true for everyone. If sexual functioning remains abnormal, this should be brought to the attention of your doctor, who will hopefully report it.

Withdrawal may reveal other continuing problems, similar to

the ongoing sexual dysfunction problem, such as memory or other problems. It is important to report these. The best way to find a remedy is to bring the problem to the attention of as many people as possible.

Dr David Healy FRCPsych
Professor of Psychological Medicine
Cardiff University

Appendix 2
The Teen Screen programme:
Mental health check-ups for youth

Teen Screen was developed first in the 1990s at Columbia University in New York. In 2003 it was endorsed by George W. Bush's New Freedom Commission on mental health, which issued a report calling for increased mental health screening. As of 2005, Teen Screen was being used in 43 of the 50 states. There is a growing concern among parents that Teen Screen is a back-door way to falsely labelling and then medicating their normal children.

1 In general, are you happy with the way things are going for you?

    Yes   Sometimes   No

2 Do you get along with your family?

    Yes   Sometimes   No

3 Do you go to school regularly?

    Yes   Sometimes   No

4 Have your grades gotten worse than they used to be?

    Yes   Sometimes   No

5 Do you have at least one adult you can really talk to?

    Yes   Sometimes   No

6 Do you get some exercise at least three times a week?

    Yes   Sometimes   No

7 Do you feel you are about the right weight for your height?

    Yes   Sometimes   No

8 Do you ever use laxatives or throw up on purpose after eating?

    Yes   Sometimes   No

9 Do you wear a seat belt in a car/truck?

    Yes   Sometimes   No

10 Do you wear a helmet when you skateboard, bicycle, motor-cycle, snowmobile, or use an ATV?

    Yes   Sometimes   No

11 Do you smoke cigarettes or chew tobacco?

    Yes   Sometimes   No

12 Do you drink alcohol?

    Yes   Sometimes   No

13 Have you tried any drugs (pot, crack, cocaine, heroin, acid, speed, etc.)?

    Yes   No

14 Do you – or does anyone you live with – have a gun or carry a gun around?

    Yes   Sometimes   No

15 Are you – or have you been – in a gang?

    Yes   No

16 Are you worried about money, a place to live, or having enough food to eat?

    Yes   Sometimes   No

17 Have you ever had sex (with women, men or both)?

    Yes   No

18 Have you ever been tested for or diagnosed with a sexually transmitted disease (herpes, gonorrhoea, chlamydia, genital warts, PID, syphilis)?

    Yes   No

19 Are you – or do you ever wonder if you are – gay, lesbian, bisexual, or transgender?

    Yes   Sometimes   No

Please re-read the italicized paragraph below before answering the following questions.

20 Have you ever had thoughts about killing yourself?

    Yes   No

21 Do you feel afraid in any of your relationships?

    Yes   No

22 Have you ever been physically or sexually abused or mistreated by anyone (kicked, hit, pushed, forced or tricked into having sex, touched on your private parts)?

    Yes   No

Notes to students taking the test

In order to help you the best we can, we would like you to answer the questions [above]. We ask all teenagers these questions because we feel they are things that affect your health and well-being. All of the questions may not fit you. You may leave blank those that do not apply to you. Please answer the questions alone, away from parents or friends, so that you can be as honest as possible.

Your answers are a confidential/private part of your medical record. However, for your safety, we are required by law to share information involving physical/sexual abuse and suicide. Every situation is individual and our staff will always talk with you before sharing any of this information.

Appendix 3

Psychiatrist's report on diagnosing children as mentally ill

A rush to medicate young minds

I have been treating, educating and caring for children for more than 30 years, half of that time as a child psychiatrist, and the changes I have seen in the practice of child psychiatry are shocking. Psychiatrists are now misdiagnosing and overmedicating children for ordinary defiance and misbehavior. The temper tantrums of belligerent children are increasingly being characterized as psychiatric illnesses.

Using such diagnoses as bipolar disorder, attention deficit hyperactivity disorder (ADHD) and Asperger's, doctors are justifying the sedation of difficult kids with powerful psychiatric drugs that may have serious, permanent or even lethal side effects.

There has been a staggering jump in the percentage of children diagnosed with a mental illness and treated with psychiatric medications. The Centers for Disease Control and Prevention reported that in 2002 almost 20 per cent of office visits to pediatricians were for psychosocial problems – eclipsing both asthma and heart disease. That same year the Food and Drug Administration reported that some 10.8 million prescriptions were dispensed for children – they are beginning to outpace the elderly in the consumption of pharmaceuticals. And this year the FDA reported that between 1999 and 2003, 19 children died after taking prescription amphetamines – the medications used to treat ADHD. These are the same drugs for which the number of prescriptions written rose 500 per cent from 1991 to 2000.

Some psychiatrists speculate that this stunning increase in childhood psychiatric disease is entirely due to improved diagnostic techniques. But setting aside the children with legitimate mental illnesses who must have psychiatric medications to function

Appendix 3

Psychiatrist's report on diagnosing children as mentally ill

A rush to medicate young minds

I have been treating, educating and caring for children for more than 30 years, half of that time as a child psychiatrist, and the changes I have seen in the practice of child psychiatry are shocking. Psychiatrists are now misdiagnosing and overmedicating children for ordinary defiance and misbehavior. The temper tantrums of belligerent children are increasingly being characterized as psychiatric illnesses.

Using such diagnoses as bipolar disorder, attention-deficit hyperactivity disorder (ADHD) and Asperger's, doctors are justifying the sedation of difficult kids with powerful psychiatric drugs that may have serious, permanent or even lethal side effects.

There has been a staggering jump in the percentage of children diagnosed with a mental illness and treated with psychiatric medications. The Centers for Disease Control and Prevention reported that in 2002 almost 20 per cent of office visits to pediatricians were for psychosocial problems – eclipsing both asthma and heart disease. That same year the Food and Drug Administration reported that some 10.8 million prescriptions were dispensed for children – they are beginning to outpace the elderly in the consumption of pharmaceuticals. And this year the FDA reported that between 1999 and 2003, 19 children died after taking prescription amphetamines – the medications used to treat ADHD. These are the same drugs for which the number of prescriptions written rose 500 per cent from 1991 to 2000.

Some psychiatrists speculate that this stunning increase in childhood psychiatric disease is entirely due to improved diagnostic techniques. But setting aside the children with legitimate mental illnesses who must have psychiatric medications to function normally, much of the increase in prescribing such medications to kids is due to the widespread use of psychiatric diagnoses to explain away the results of poor parenting practices. According to psychiatrist Jennifer Harris, quoted in the January/February issue of *Psychotherapy Networker*, 'Many clinicians find it easier to tell parents their child has a brain-based disorder than to suggest parenting changes.'

Parents and teachers today seem to believe that any boy who wriggles in his seat and wilfully defies his teacher's rules has ADHD. Likewise, any child who has a temper tantrum is diagnosed with bipolar disorder. After all, an anger outburst is how most parents define a 'mood swing'. Contributing to this widespread problem of misdiagnosis is the doctor's willingness to accept, without question, the assessment offered by a parent or teacher.

What was once a somber, heart-wrenching decision for a parent and something children often resisted – medicating a child's mind – has now become a widely used technique in parenting a belligerent child. As if they were debating parental locks on the home computer or whether to allow a co-ed sleepover, parents now share notes with each other about whose child is taking what pill for which diagnosis.

These days parents cruise the Internet, take self-administered surveys, diagnose their children and choose a medication before they ever set foot in the psychiatrist's office. If the first doctor doesn't prescribe what you want, the next one will.

There was a time in the profession of child psychiatry when doctors insisted on hours of evaluation of a child before making a diagnosis or prescribing a medication. Today some of my colleagues in psychiatry brag that they can make an initial assessment of a child and write a prescription in less than 20 minutes. Some parents tell me it took their pediatrician only five minutes. Who's the winner in this race? Unfortunately, when a child is diagnosed with a mental illness, almost everyone benefits. The schools get more state funding for the education of a mentally handicapped student. Teachers have more subdued students in their already overcrowded classrooms. Finally, parents are not forced to examine their poor parenting practices, because they have the perfect excuse: Their child has a chemical imbalance.

The only loser in this equation is the child. It is the child who must endure the side effects of these powerful drugs and be burdened unnecessarily with the label of a mental illness. Medicating a child, based on a misdiagnosis, is a tragic injustice for the child: His or her only advocate is the parent who lacked the courage to apply appropriate discipline.

Well-intentioned but misinformed teachers, parents using the Internet to diagnose their children, and hurried doctors are all a part of the complex system that drives the current practice of mis-diagnosing and overmedicating children. The solution lies in the practice of good, conscientious medicine that is careful, thorough and patient-centered.

Parents need to be more careful with whom they entrust their child's mental health care. Doctors need to take the time to understand their pediatric patients better and have the courage to deliver the bad news that sometimes a child's disruptive, aggressive and defiant behavior is due to poor parenting, not to a chemical imbalance such as bipolar disorder or ADHD.

Elizabeth J. Roberts, Washington Post, *Sunday 8 October 2006, B07*
© *2006 The Washington Post Company*

Elizabeth J. Roberts is a child and adolescent psychiatrist in California and the author of *Should You Medicate Your Child's Mind?*

Useful addresses

Helpful contacts

James Nayler Foundation
Unit B6
Spithead Industrial Estate
Shanklin
Isle of Wight PO33 9PH
Tel.: 01983 401700
Website: www.truthtrustconsent.com
Email: admin@truthtrustconsent.com

An independent charity set up in 1999, and to 'advance education in the causes and treatment of personality disorders and to relieve the suffering caused by such disorders'. The foundation is in the process of developing the following: an emotion support centre, with face-to-face, telephone and online support for those suffering emotional distress; education, research and training programmes to support those working to relieve this suffering; and an information base, communications, network, conferences, workshops and publications.

International Center for the Study of Psychiatry and Psychology, Inc. (ICSPP)
www.icspp.org

Based in the USA, this non-profit research and educational network of professionals and lay people has been in existence for 30 years; they inform other professionals, media and the public about the potential dangers of biological theories and treatments in psychiatry.

International Coalition for Drug Awareness (ICFDA)
www.drugawareness.org

This is a consumer watchdog in the USA and raises public awareness of the adverse reactions patients may experience when taking SSRI antidepressants. They run another website which is a collection of news stories and articles collected by two ICFDA directors: www.ssristories.com

Finding a therapist

If you require a fully registered psychotherapist you can contact the following organizations:

British Association for Counselling and Psychotherapy (BACP)
BACP House
15 St John's Business Park
Lutterworth
Leicestershire LE17 4HB
Tel.: 0870 443 5252
Website: www.bacp.co.uk

British Psychoanalytic Council
West Hill House
6 Swains Lane
London N6 6QS
Tel.: 020 7267 3626
Website: www.bcp.org.uk
Email: mail@psychoanalytic-council.org

British Psychological Society
St Andrew's House
48 Princess Road East
Leicester LE1 7DR
Tel.: 0116 254 9568
Website: www.bps.org.uk

UK Council for Psychotherapy (UKCP)
2nd Floor, Edward House
2 Wakley Street
London EC1V 7LT
Website: www.psychotherapy.org.uk
Email: info@psychotherapy.org.uk

Other organizations and websites

UK

British Association for Behavioural and Cognitive Psychotherapies (BABCP)
The Globe Centre
P.O. Box 9
Accrington BB5 0XB
Tel.: 01254 875277
Website: www.babcp.com
A multidisciplinary interest group for people involved in the practice and theory of these particular psychotherapies.

Calipso
www.calipso.co.uk
Provides mental-health training materials, using cognitive behavioural therapy, for healthcare professionals, and self-help materials for use with patients.

Compassionate Friends, The (TCF)
53 North Street
Bristol BS3 1EN
Tel.: 0845 120 3785
Website: www.tcf.org.uk

Depression Alliance
212 Spitfire Studios
63–71 Collier Street
London N1 9BE
Tel.: 0845 123 23 20
Website: www.depressionalliance.org
Email: information@depressionalliance.org

This is the leading UK charity for people with depression, working to relieve and prevent this treatable condition by providing information, support services and understanding to people affected by it. Depression Alliance has three offices within the UK. You can contact their regional information lines via the main phone number.

Jewish Association for the Mentally Ill (JAMI)
16A North End Road
London NW11 7PH
Tel.: 020 8458 2223
Website: www.jamiuk.org
Email: info@jamiuk.org

MDF The Bipolar Organization (formerly Manic Depression Fellowship)
Castle Works
21 St George's Road
London SE1 6ES
Tel.: 08456 340 540 (UK)
00 44 207 793 2600 (rest of world)
Website: www.mdf.org.uk

Medical and Healthcare products Regulatory Agency (MHRA)
Website: www.mhra.gov.uk

MIND (National Association for Mental Health)
15–19 Broadway
London E15 4BQ
Tel.: 020 8522 1728
MindinfoLine: 0845 766 0163 (9.15 a.m. to 5.15 p.m., Monday to Friday)
Website: www.mind.org.uk
A website in the Channel Islands provides mental health information:
www.mindinfo.co.uk

National Mental Health Drugs Helpline
020 7919 2999 (11 a.m. to 5 p.m., Monday to Friday)

Provides independent advice and information about mental health drugs.

National Phobics Society
Zion Community Resource Centre
339 Stretford Road
Hulme
Manchester M15 4ZY
Tel.: 0870 122 2325
Website: www.phobics-society.org.uk

Outside In (Cambridge) Ltd
3 The Links
Trafalgar Way
Bar Hill
Cambridge CB3 8UD
Tel.: 01954 780 500
Website: www.outsidein.co.uk

Provides information on seasonal affective disorder and their online shop
carries a range of products including light boxes.

PANTS UK
Email: pants.uk@virgin.net

Help from the author on antidepressants and withdrawal.

PAPYRUS
Lodge House, Thompson Park
Ormerod Road
Burnley
Lancs. BB11 2RU
Tel.: 01282 432777
Website: www.papyrus-uk.org

A UK national charity which works towards the prevention of suicide,
especially among young people.

Rethink
5th Floor, Royal London House
22–25 Finsbury Square
London EC2A 1DX
Tel.: 0845 456 0455
National Advice Service line: 020 8974 6814 (10 a.m. to 3 p.m., Monday to Friday)
Website: www.rethink.org
Email: advice@rethink.org

Australia

Black Dog Institute
Hospital Road
Prince of Wales Hospital
Randwick
New South Wales 2031
Tel.: (02) 9382 4530 (9 a.m. to 5 p.m., Monday to Friday)
Website: www.blackdoginstitute.org.au
Email: blackdog@unsw.edu.au

Founded in 2002, the Institute's mission is to advance the understanding, diagnosis and management of mood disorders by continually raising clinical, research, education and training standards. In so doing, the Institute aims to improve the lives of those affected, and in turn, the lives of their families and friends.

Ireland

Depression Dialogues
2 Eden Park
Dun Laoghaire
Dublin
Republic of Ireland
Tel. 01 2800084
Website: www.depressiondialogues.ie

Irish Association of Suicidology
16 New Antrim Street
Castlebar
Co. Mayo
Ireland
Tel.: +353 94 9250858
Website: www.ias.ie

US websites

Associated Psychological Health Services (based in Wisconsin)
www.abcmedsfree.com

Food and Drug Administration (FDA)
www.fda.gov

Public Library of Science
www.plos.org

An international non-profit organization of scientists and physicians committed to making the world's scientific and medical literature a freely available public resource. Its core principles are: open access; excellence; scientific integrity; breadth; cooperation; financial fairness; community engagement; internationalism; and science as a public resource. Its headquarters is in the United States, and there are offices around the world.

References and further reading

Alexander, F. G. and Selesnick, S. T. (1966) *The History of Psychiatry*. Harper and Row.

Breggin, Peter R. and Cohen, David (1999) *Your Drug May Be Your Problem: How and Why to Stop Taking Psychiatric Medication*. HarperCollins.

Burns, David D. (1990) *The Feeling Good Handbook*. Plume/Penguin.

Butler, G. and Hope, T. (1995) *Manage Your Mind: The Mental Fitness Guide*. Oxford University Press.

Cantopher, Dr Tim (2006) *Depressive Illness: The Curse of the Strong* (2nd edn). Sheldon Press.

Caplan, Paula J. (1995) *They Say You're Crazy: How the World's Most Powerful Psychiatrists Decide Who's Normal*. Perseus Books.

Chernow, Barbara A. and Vallasi, George A., eds (1993) *The Columbia Encyclopedia* (5th edn). Columbia University Press.

Cheung, Theresa (2006) *The Depression Diet Book*. Sheldon Press.

Corry, Dr Michael and Tubridy, Dr Áine (2005) *Depression: An Emotion not a Disease*. Mercier Press.

Didion, Joan (2005) *The Year of Magical Thinking*, Fourth Estate.

Geary, Amanda (2001) *The Food and Mood Handbook*. Thorsons.

Gelder, M., Gath, D., Mayou, R. and Cowen, P. (1998) *Oxford Textbook of Psychiatry* (3rd revised edn). Oxford University Press.

Glenmullen, Joseph (2000) *Prozac Backlash*. Simon & Schuster.

Glenmullen, Joseph (2005), *The Antidepressant Solution*. Free Press.

Greenberger, Dennis and Padesky, Christine A. (1995) *Mind over Mood*. Guilford Press.

Healy, David (1997) *The Anti-depressant Era*. Harvard University Press.

Healy, David (2002), *Psychiatric Drugs Explained* (3rd edn). Elsevier Science.

Healy, David (2003) *Let Them Eat Prozac*. Lorimer.

Hill, K. (1995) *The Long Sleep: Young People and Suicide*. Virago.

Hunter, R. Lanny and Hunter, Victor L. (2004) *What Your Doctor and Your Pastor Want you to Know about Depression*. Chalice Press.

Hurcombe, Linda (2004) *Losing a Child: Explorations in Grief*. Sheldon Press.

Jamison, Kay Redfield (1995) *An Unquiet Mind: A Memoir of Moods and Madness*. A. A. Knopf.

Johnson, Dr Bob (2002) *Emotional Health: What Emotions Are and How They Cause Social and Mental Diseases*. Trust Consent Publishing (PO Box 49, Ventnor, Isle of Wight PO38 9AA).

Johnson, Dr Bob (2006) *Unsafe at Any Dose: Exposing Psychiatric Dogma*. Trust Consent Publishing (as above).

Law, Jacky (2006) *Big Pharma: How the World's Biggest Drug Companies Control Illness*. Constable and Robinson.

Lynch, Terry (2004) *Beyond Prozac: Healing Mental Distress.* PCCS Books.

Medawar, Charles and Hardon, Anita (2004) *Medicines Out of Control? Antidepressants and the Conspiracy of Goodwill.* Aksant Academic Publishers.

Office for National Statistics (2004). See <www.mentalhealth.org.uk/information>.

O'Meara, Kelly Patricia (2006) *Psyched Out: How Psychiatry Sells Mental Illness and Pushes Pills That Kill.* AuthorHouse.

Peck, M. Scott (1978) *The Road Less Travelled.* Simon & Schuster.

Peters, Dr Michael, ed. (2002) *The British Medical Association Illustrated Medical Dictionary.* Dorling Kindersley.

Pierce, D. W. (1981) 'Suicidal intent in self-injury. The predictive validation of a suicide intent scale: a five year follow-up', *British Journal of Psychiatry*, 139: 391–6.

Porter, Roy (1997) *The Greatest Benefit to Mankind: A Medical History of Humanity from Antiquity to the Present.* Fontana.

Roberts, Elizabeth J. (2006) *Should You Medicate Your Child's Mind?* Marlowe and Company.

Rowe, Dorothy (2001) *Depression: The Way Out of Your Prison.* Brunner-Routledge.

Saunders, Naomi (2006) *Simplify Your Life: Downsize and De-stress.* Sheldon Press.

Schneidman, Dr Edwin (2004) *The Suicidal Mind.* Oxford University Press.

Searle, Ruth (2007) *The Thinking Person's Guide to Happiness.* Sheldon Press.

Shorter, Edward (1998) *A History of Psychiatry.* John Wiley.

Stannard, Russell, ed. (2000) *God for the 21st Century.* Templeton Foundation Press.

Trickett, Shirley (2001) *Coping with Anxiety and Depression.* Sheldon Press.

Tugendhat, Julia (2005) *Living with Loss and Grief.* Sheldon Press.

Vincent, Paul (2005) *50 Things You Can Do Today to Beat Depression.* Upfront Publishing.

Whitaker, Robert (2002) *Mad in America.* Perseus Publishing.

Whitaker, Robert (2005) 'Anatomy of an epidemic: Psychiatric drugs and the astonishing rise of mental illness in America', *Ethical Human Psychology and Psychiatry*, 7(1).

Index